2004

Pianos and Pianism

*Frederic Horace Clark and the
Quest for Unity of
Mind, Body, and Universe*

Robert Andres

The Scarecrow Press, Inc.
Lanham, Maryland, and London
2001

SCARECROW PRESS, INC.

Published in the United States of America
by Scarecrow Press, Inc.
4720 Boston Way, Lanham, Maryland 20706
www.scarecrowpress.com

4 Pleydell Gardens, Folkestone
Kent CT20 2DN, England

British Library Cataloguing-in-Publication Information Available

Library of Congress Cataloging-in-Publication Data

Andres, Robert, 1959–
    Pianos and pianism : Frederic Horace Clark and the quest for unity of mind, body, and universe / Robert Andres.
        p. cm.
    Includes bibliographical references and index.
    ISBN 0-8108-4046-4 (alk. paper)
        1. Clark, Frederic Horace, 1860–1917—Criticism and interpretation. 2. Piano—Instruction and study. 3. Piano—Construction. I. Title.
    ML423.C65 A53 2001
    786.2'092—dc21
    [B]   2001020691

To Honor, who was with me when it counted.

Contents

List of Figures   vii

Foreword   ix

Preface   xi

Introduction   xiii

1   The Life of Frederic Horace Clark   1

2   Anna Steiniger's Life and Education   27

3   Clark's Writings   37

4   The Religion and the Science of the
    "Cherubim-Doctrine" and of the *Harmonie*   55

5   The New Technique   65

6   The *Harmonie*-piano: "Soul-Mirror"   75

7   The Philosophy of Pure Pianism and Its Consequences   83

8   The Three Impromptus Op. 4:
    A Compendium of the Clark-Steiniger Piano School   95

9 Clark and His Contemporaries   103

10 Today's Perspective   119

11 Conclusion   125

Appendix A F. H. Clark's Concert Programs   129

Appendix B F. H. Clark's Impromptu
            Op. 4 No. 3 "Hiawatha"   135

Appendix C F. H. Clark's Edition of
            Six Etudes by Cramer   143

Bibliography   151

Index   157

About the Author   163

List of Figures

5.1. An illustration of proportions in a rotating
      system, after Figure 8 in *Die Lehre*   69

7.1. An "envelopment"   84

8.1. Impromptu 1, measures 5-8 and 13-16   99

Foreword

It is a brave writer who sets out on a detailed study of a figure who has been largely dismissed and whose chronology is anything but organized. Firstly, out of the many versions of Frederic Horace Clark's life, here is a rational and wholly believable account, devoid of the many contradictions to be found in other versions. Indeed, one only gets as far as discovering that what we think of as the somewhat trite *Grande Galop chromatique* could have had such an impact on Clark that the urge is to go further and find out what this impact led to. In fact, his determination to meet Liszt was such that he left his home immediately and embarked on what was to be an almost impossible journey to find Liszt. The reasons for the number of places he visited are chronicled in this book, but it seems that after reaching Weimar he learned that Liszt was in Rome. After a matter of months, during which he nearly died from cold in a mountain pass, he reached Rome, only to find that on finally meeting Liszt he was unable to speak; when Liszt departed for Sorrento. Clark was determined to catch up with him, and did so after a journey of almost a year, nearly all on foot. The details are, however, uncertain, and although they should be read, the most probable chronology is explained on page 5 onward.

We come into the realm of the talked-about *Music Study in Germany*, written by Amy Fay, who advised Clark to study with Ludwig Deppe, the last teacher mentioned in her book in somewhat glowing terms. Other reactions to Deppe were not so enthusiastic, and Liszt, who had apparently known him for several years, clearly wanted nothing to do with him. In 1832 Clark decided to formulate a "psycho-physical" system of playing, and produced a series of "transcendental etudes" which he dedicated to Liszt. Obviously these were tied up with Clark's research and scientific study, which Deppe virtually dismissed in favor of his own finger exercises.

The central part of this book deals with the *Harmonie*, of the body and soul, and the many experiments to achieve this. An early one was to play the piano standing up, with the keyboard elevated to shoulder height. The *Harmonie*-piano itself was later designed with curved keycaps and two keyboards; the details of this twenty-five-year development are discussed here in considerable detail, as is the philosophy of piano music, the raison d'être of these many experiments. It would seem that the piano itself would be designed in order that the player would bear the least amount of physical movement, allowing the thoughts and inspirations to pass through him without impediment. I cannot resist commenting that in this age we see and hear many pianists who play against the piano (as something to be conquered) and the result has little to do with musical ideas. If the instrument is part of oneself—one's voice, if you like—then there is no restriction on the ideas that should go in a straight line to the instrument that will express them.

Personally, I have certain reservations as to the necessity of redesigning the piano in the way that Clark saw it, but then very little had been said about the playing and philosophy being linked, and this was possibly the result of the first major awareness of this link. To read it in all its detail is something of a revelation, but it is also an intense study of all the available details that have been put together so painstakingly and so convincingly.

Dr. Peter Katin
Professor, Royal College of Music, London

Preface

More than twenty years ago I acquired, by pure chance, a book by Frederic Horace Clark in a used book store in Zagreb, Croatia. The title of the book was *Liszts Offenbarung*. This was the beginning of a chain of events further spurred by my doctoral studies in piano in the United States. The more I discovered about the author and his work, the more I became convinced that the time had come to delve into research of his achievements. Enough time has now elapsed to allow a modern investigator to attempt an assessment of Clark's work and his place in the history of the development of piano technique.

I sincerely hope that my attempt will at least partially correct the injustice done to Clark, who has been constantly, and almost without exception, rejected, criticized, and neglected by performers and musicologists alike.

I wish to express my deepest gratitude for his unwavering and constructive help to my mentor at the University of Kansas, now retired, Dr. J. Bunker Clark; to pianist Mario Feninger, of Los Angeles, for support and some important words of advice; to Prof. Christian Spring, of Maur, Switzerland, who has gone to immense trouble to secure some vital documents concerning Clark's biography; to Anna Pia Maissen Zeltner and Dr. Robert Dünki, of the Zurich City Archives, for deciphering the handwriting of the original documents; to Öffentliche Bibliothek der Universität Basel and to the Haags Gemeentemuseum; and finally to my lucky star that made me buy a book by Frederic Horace Clark years ago, long before I ever realized the book's importance, or imagined the future activity it would cause.

Introduction

A person who lives his whole life under a self-imposed set of rules of conduct, work, and even thinking, who spends a substantial part of his life as a vegetarian, who abstains from sexual relationship for several months right after being married (following the biblical code), who devotes his whole life to the development of an idea, who ignores hardships and rejection in favor of inner peace and contentment—such a person could be called many names, including naive, unrealistic, crazed, or fanatic. But Frederic Horace Clark could also be one of the selected few in history who had a real message for humanity, however obscured and incongruous it might have seemed at the time. If so, he is definitely also one of the majority of those special people whom humanity chose to overlook.

If it is feasible to strip an author of the complexity of his personal idiosyncrasies, however necessary they might prove to be for the actual formation of his work, then Clark has to be regarded as a highly prolific writer and musician, whose ideas were truly ahead of his time. He actually started many of the developments in the comprehensive field of piano technique, study, and interpretation of the twentieth century. His greatest mistake was probably the refusal or lack of capacity to make himself more understood. Being for the greater part of his life totally immersed into his ideas, Clark apparently, and ironically, forgot to take a wider perspective of humanity and the age he lived in, to make his thoughts more accessible to the general musician—ironically, because he was the one to urge humanity to observe itself in a universal context. It is also possible that his uncompromising spirit and stubbornness prevented him from "spelling out" his message, a procedure that would possibly oversimplify his thought, blunt its impact, and compromise its universal character. If so, it is unfortunate that his own character was an obstacle to a wider acceptance of his ideas, even though it was those same personal traits that probably made his work possible. Although many of his ideas have already been adopted and perfected by others, there are still some universal aspects of his doctrine that should appeal to the contemporary pianist and musician in general. Perhaps it is now time to cast away old prejudice, forgive Clark his unrelenting character, and, in this age of global awareness and cross-communication of cultural diversity, remember his ideas for the benefit of all humanity.

1

The Life of Frederic Horace Clark

In his conversation with the pianist Bettina Walker, Frederic(k) Horace Clark(e) (-Steiniger), known also under his literary pseudonym as "Leo(pold) St. Damian," related that his family made a clearing in the heart of a large forest area, "one of the loneliest and most isolated spots you could imagine"[1] to build a home. Born on December 23, 1858,[2] Clark was the youngest in the second or third generation of children born in Liebeshain, a lonely settlement in a forest area, supposedly three days' walk west of Chicago.[3] His father was apparently a very important person in the railroad enterprise.[4] Some of Clark's older sisters lived for a couple of years with some relatives and had the opportunity to learn the basic principles of piano playing. When they returned home, their parents purchased an old square piano, and it provided Clark's first encounter with music. Until his seventh birthday he was actually prepared by his grandmother for a life of priesthood, and from this early age Clark's life was intertwined with and ingrained in religion. When his grandmother left to live in her own residence, his aunt briefly led him through his initial musical training. Soon after, she married a priest and moved to Pittsburgh, Pennsylvania.[5] Clark continued to learn about music by himself. By the age of twelve, he had mastered the usual waltzes, potpourris, and similar music in his sisters' repertory, and added to those a substantial number of pieces by Bach, Mozart, Beethoven, and Mendelssohn, acquired by chance. On the fourth of July in 1874 his aunt sent him a relatively large amount of printed music, mostly transcriptions, but also Beethoven's "Moonlight Sonata" and Liszt's *Grande Galop chromatique*.[6]

The impact Liszt's music had upon him was immense, draining him of all emotion and leaving him ill and powerless for five days.[7] According to his own words in his book *Liszts Offenbarung*[8] he felt the immense gap between everyday life and the richness of the spiritual contents found in a work of art. Catching a glimpse of this through Liszt's work, he became obsessed with the discrepancy and sought the advice of his granduncle who lived for twenty years in a cave by Liebeshain, apparently as a hermit.[9]

The reassurance Clark received from his granduncle completely convinced him of the compatibility of music making and religion, in light of the adherence or deviation from religious doctrine when involved in music. However, upon explaining to his grandmother his determination to pursue a musical career, he was severely rebuked because, according to her—she was obviously fervently obsessed with religion—music was a vice and not a blessing. Confronted with this stern opinion, Clark fled his home for Chicago, where he stayed with a German family who was for years friends of the Clarks. From them he learned that Liszt lived in Germany, the place where "all great people live."[10] The next day Clark got a job as a piano player in a bar, and the following day his parents came to beg him to return home. Having shown his firm determination to travel to Germany, he convinced his parents to help him and he moved to Pittsburgh to his aunt's house, where he gave piano lessons and saved funds for the ticket to Rotterdam.

Sailing for sixteen days, he was influenced by some of his new acquaintances[11] to start his study in Leipzig, where he happened to arrive on the day of the entrance examination (without having played for at least eighteen days).[12] The jury, consisting of Louis Maas, Ernst Wenzel, Oscar Paul,[13] and a Prof. Schleinitz almost did not allow him to play Liszt's "Chromatic Gallop." They probably thought the boy had overestimated himself and, besides, they would certainly have preferred a classical piece. Therefore, they interrupted him quickly and gave him a sonata by Mozart to sight-read. Clark felt an enormous tension during the unpleasant exam and ran out right after he finished. A porter convinced him to return and wait for the decision. On his way back, however, he ran into a music shop and talked to the owner, who happened to be the famous publisher Christian Friedrich Kahnt.[14] Kahnt was an admirer of Liszt and gave him a letter of recommendation for the master. Without even waiting for the jury's decision, Clark proceeded right away on foot to Weimar. This trip he accomplished in three days.[15]

Upon arrival there Clark learned that Liszt was in Rome at the time, and was bitterly disappointed, but immediately proceeded to his new destination. He needed at least seven weeks to reach Munich, and then five more before he came before Passo di Stelvio (Stilfserjoch), a mountain pass he chose to cross the Alps. However, the peasants from the village of Trafoi strongly advised him against any attempt to pass since snowstorms and bad weather had been almost ceaseless for three months, this being the time of the winter solstice. No guide would take him more than three miles toward the top across the seven-meter-deep snow. By this time, however, he was so determined that he decided to put his destiny into the Lord's hands. Speculating that he would pass if the Lord deemed him worthy of becoming a musician, or otherwise freeze in the snow, he left on his own. Soon the telegraph posts, which he was following, disappeared completely under the snow, and the tunnel that he should have gone through was also completely buried. He continued for about three hours and then succumbed to exhaustion and cold, losing his consciousness to the "white death."

He woke up after forty-eight hours in a Trafoi inn, saved by two mountain guides, and with severe freeze burns. After recovering, he was forced by the villagers to take the post road to Brenner Pass, and he pretended to obey them, only to use the first possible chance to detour to the Passo di Stelvio and try it again at any cost. He crossed the Swiss border at the village of Santa Maria, and continued during the night all the way to the observatory at the top of Monte Stelvio, which was then, according to Clark, the highest human settlement in Europe. He descended the Italian side of the Alps to (Bad) Bormio. On his way to Lago di Como, he became increasingly disturbed by the distance of his goal, which did not seem to get any closer. As a consequence, he fell sick and lost several more days there. Reaching Milan, he met an English painter, John Ruskin, at the door of the cathedral.[16] This encounter, during which Clark was invited to lunch, was his first opportunity to speak English after quite some time. He began to feel uncomfortable surrounded by the Italian people and culture of which he knew little. Traveling at top speed, he finally reached Rome at the end of June. Clark actually encountered Liszt, in his priest's attire, but was so shaken by the moment that he failed to address the master. Waiting in vain for Liszt to return, Clark found out that the *abbé* had left for Sorrento, a town near Naples. Completing this final stretch of the journey,

Clark at last caught up with Liszt. According to *Liszts Offenbarung*, this journey began in Chicago in early September, and ended in Sorrento, probably some time in mid to late August. There is no information on the duration of the last part of the journey, from Rome to Sorrento, but calculating his average speed, it had to be around two months. The total time of the trip adds up to approximately 360 days, nearly a full year, 325 days of which Clark traveled on foot.[17]

Naturally, Liszt was amazed at the strain Clark had undergone to reach him. He listened to the whole story and decided to take the young pilgrim with him back to Germany—his departure had already been set for the next day.[18] Clark promised that he would stay with Liszt for eight days, and upon their return to Weimar, Liszt arranged for him to stay at the *Zum Adler* (At the eagle) inn. During his stay in Weimar, Clark had several long conversations with Liszt. Those conversations, the contents of which takes up almost half of the book *Liszts Offenbarung*, represent the only contribution Clark was ever remembered for by posterity, and their truthfulness has been questioned. They will be described and evaluated in detail in subsequent chapters. Upon Liszt's insistence, Clark returned to Leipzig and the conservatory at the end of September. From the window of his lodging in the Klostergasse,[19] he could see the Marktplatz, the old town hall, and the Thomaskirche, where Bach used to work. With interruptions, Clark studied in Germany for seven years. During that time, he returned twice to America, and often visited Liszt in Weimar.

This whole period is chronologically very unclear and allows several interpretations. In *My Musical Experiences*, Clark is quoted as having earned his diploma in two and a half years. He then returned to America, found a position as an organist, and worked for the following "three or four" years, studying on his own and playing piano recitals at the same time.[20] Feeling dissatisfied, he returned to Germany and almost at once met Ludwig Deppe, a renowned German piano teacher.[21]

Another source indicates, however, that he studied with Prof. Oscar Paul in Leipzig from 1876 to 1879.[22] This directly contradicts his claim of meeting Liszt for the first time in 1877, unless the whole "pilgrimage" episode is disregarded, in which case he might have met him while already a student. In any case, he was then sent to America because of weakness in his upper body, spent some time there in 1880[23] (and 1881?), and returned "soon after" to resume his studies, this time with Prof. Ehrlich in Berlin.

The above reference in *My Musical Experiences* notwithstanding, there are no details in any of his books concerning a second trip to

America, before his marriage. In *Liszts Offenbarung* he mentions studying again with Dr. Paul at the end of the seven-year period and only there contends that he went to Deppe, with the specific intention of trying to influence Deppe's mind and change his theory of piano playing.

It is interesting to note that Clark was present when Miss Bettina Walker played the first time for Deppe. She mentions meeting him when he had already been married to Anna Steiniger for several months, and studying with Deppe for a year and three months. Assuming he started with Deppe in the fall of 1881, and taking the previously mentioned statements by Walker into account, Bettina Walker probably met Deppe and Clark in the late fall or early winter of 1882.

It is probable that the above mention of 1876 as his first year of study in Germany is an error. However, bearing in mind that Clark was born two years earlier than was commonly known, the previously obvious count according to which he started studying in Germany in the fall of 1877 or spring of 1878, graduated from the Leipzig Conservatory after two and a half years at the end of 1879 or in the spring of 1880, and then spent three or four years in America, might have to be revised. If all the events were to be moved two years earlier (the difference between 1860, as commonly known, and 1858 as his true year of birth), this would eliminate the discrepancy of two years that is encountered when organizing the chronology of his life. It adds to the confusion, though, regarding the date of his presumable meeting with Liszt. The fact that in several instances he insists on some dates that allow for both chronologies to be possible makes it virtually impossible to discern which one is correct. According to *Liszts Offenbarung*, he was back in Germany by 1883 or 1884, although in the same book he mentions visiting Liszt in Weimar in the spring of 1882. It is also certain that Walker had met him in Berlin in 1882 and that he got married in the same year.

The only apparent solution is either to attribute these inaccuracies to erratic memory, given the time lapse, or to try to establish a most probable chronology. Based on Clark being born in 1858, it could continue with his move to Pittsburgh, Pennsylvania, at the age of twelve, and crossing the ocean to Hamburg at the age of sixteen. Consequently, in 1874 he must have started his pilgrimage to Italy, which ended sometime in the late summer of 1875. This chronology might loosely support the year 1876 as the beginning of his piano lessons in Leipzig. He took his diploma in two and a half years, and returned to America for two or three years, during which he was teaching and practicing. He came back to Germany in 1881, where he studied with Ehrlich,[24] and possibly also with Moritz Moszkowski (Kullak's school), Oscar Raif (Tausig's student), and Paul, and then finally with Deppe. At an uncertain date, Clark also answered an invitation by a Russian baroness to visit her at her estates in Tartu, now Estonian but until 1917 a Russian town.[25] Clark met there Prof. Gustav Teichmüller,[26] who influenced Clark very much, especially with his works *Neue Psychologie, Philosophie der Liebe*, and *Philosophie der Unsterblichkeit.* During Clark's last visit to Chicago, "a female student of Liszt and Deppe" tried to convince him to continue his studies with Ludwig Deppe instead of Paul. In Walker's book, Clark described himself as lucky to have heard about Deppe in Germany, and be admitted to his class. Amy Fay, the American "female student," disagreed, however, that Clark had heard about Deppe in Germany, as W. S. B. Mathews had reported in his journal *Music.*[27]

In a letter to the journal, she stated that Clark had read her book *Music Study in Germany*[28] while in America and wanted further information about Deppe before leaving for the second time for Europe.[29] She advised Clark to take lessons from Deppe and his assistant, Fräulein Steiniger. Amy Fay then, according to Clark, sent him a book to be delivered to Deppe. When delivering the book, Clark first met Anna Steiniger, Deppe's student. The "magnetic undercurrent that characterized the playing of that teacher's foremost pupil" fascinated him[30] and soon they were married.

The whole episode is described in greater detail, and with some discrepancies, in *Iphigenia.* According to this, Deppe was called upon by a young man (Clark was named in *Iphigenia* Leo[pold] St. Damian), whom he met at Taubert's recital on Easter Eve of 1881.[31] Deppe related that event to Anna during one of their customary walks, this one being on an April evening in 1881, only a day or two after her birthday. At the time Clark was apparently the chaperone of a young American boy traveling across Europe. According to *Brahms' Noblesse* and Cobb, he was also taking piano lessons from Ehrlich, the following month from Raif, and occasionally from Moszkowski. Two days after the conversation, Deppe brought Clark to Anna's house for a visit. Only after that did Clark attend one of her private concert-soirées, entering during the first movement of Beethoven's Fourth Sonata. Her maid and mother were soon discussing the "American youth falling in love with Anna."[32] After the summer, which she spent in Thuringia, Anna returned during the last week of September. Right upon her return, she was surprised by a visit from Leo (Clark) and his American friend.

In the course of the visit, Clark recounted his latest travels. He referred to part of it as done "in the same way that I traveled once alone from Berlin [?] to Naples when a boy of sixteen, and after first arriving in Europe."[33] He also included an interesting (if true) event: after visiting the "Wagner series" (probably Bayreuth) he met Dr. Paul, who got angry at the mention of Deppe. Later, in Weimar, Clark met Liszt and they departed together to Zurich, where they saw Deppe. Clark stated that Deppe knew Liszt for several years, but Liszt also turned his back on Clark upon hearing of Deppe. When Clark tried to take Liszt's hand to kiss it, as he usually did before departure, Liszt apparently struck him on the lips, causing some bleeding.[34]

That fall, Deppe allowed Anna to start teaching Clark herself. Clark was invited to her house for Christmas, thus breaking her ten-year-old habit of having only her mother and Deppe for the holiday. On New Year's Day (Sunday), Clark visited her again and proposed to her. Anna took eight weeks to deliberate, having doubts mainly because of the difference in their ages (she was 12 years older). They were betrothed on George Washington's birthday, February 22. However, apparently because he could furnish no written proof that he had ever been born, the strict German rules made them travel to England for the wedding ceremony.[35] They were married on Easter Monday of 1882, almost exactly one year after they met for the first time, in St. John's Church in Bloomsbury, London. Being Catholics, they were able to take communion there.

Their wedding trip took them through Munich, Tyrol, and Italy. They passed through Weimar where, regardless of his wife's hesitation and unwillingness, Clark introduced her to Liszt. Partly because of Clark's eagerness and overexcitement, partly because his wife always appeared stern and restrained, and probably also due to Liszt's advanced age and impatience, as soon as Clark mentioned the name Deppe, Liszt threw down the music which she gave him and left the room without a word.[36] Regardless of this incident, the Clarks spent a happy summer and fall, wandering through Tyrol and Italy.

In the winter of the same year (1882), Clark renewed his efforts in the research of physiology, physics, metaphysics, and theology. He took some of these courses at the Berlin University, trying to formulate a "psycho-physical system" of piano playing, which he wanted to present to Liszt. In the meantime, Clark also sent anonymously his "Transcendental etudes" to Liszt through the already mentioned Russian

baroness. Having learned that Liszt spoke favorably of them, Clark
sent him another copy, this time with a dedication, to which Liszt replied with a postcard, accepting it.[37]

This was also a period in which Clark and his wife were introduced to Hermann Grimm by Russian baroness Emilie von Tiesenhauser-Manteuffel, whom they had met in Livonia. The baroness was
married to Baron von Tesse and had an estate near Riga.[38] Gisela
Grimm, Hermann Grimm's wife, was the daughter of Bettina von
Arnim, who is known by the letter exchange she had as a child with
Goethe, and also by her friendship with Beethoven.[39] Gisela abdicated
in order to marry Hermann Grimm, son of one of the Grimms who
wrote the German fairy tales.[40] Grimm, in turn, introduced Clark to
Hermann Helmholtz and Prof. Reuleaux (the author of *Kinematics*).[41]
The Grimms supported Clark's research and scientific study. This of-
fended Deppe, who thought that one "should devote one's entire day
to the practice of his finger-exercises."[42]

In May 1885, while walking and praying in the old palace gardens near the mausoleum of Queen Louise in Charlottenburg, where
they lived, Clark experienced a "divine revelation."[43] He suddenly
grasped the basis of his new system of piano playing, and at once
stood up decisively against all methods based on mechanical and anti-
anatomical principles.[44] In the same month he published his first conclusions in Charlottenburg's *Intelligenz-Blatt*. At about the same time
his wife published an article in *Lessmans Zeitung* on *Eutonie*.[45] According to Clark, the famous—indeed, the only—article published by
Deppe, entitled *Armleiden des Klavierspielers* was a reaction to the
first of these articles, and to the request by Steiniger and her colleague
Antonia Bandmann that Deppe amend his terminology.[46] In the early
summer of 1885 Clark traveled to Weimar to see Liszt, for what he felt
would be the last time.[47] Making a detour through Jena, he met there
and conversed with Rudolf Eucken, a philosopher, and Westphal (first
name not mentioned by Clark), a philologist.[48] Both of them were writing on the relationship of the soul and religion to art, as well as on the
contrast of natural and metronomically leveled proportions of tempos
in a musical form. In August of the same year Clark published in Berlin his fully expanded and anatomically based system of piano playing,
under the title *Lehre des einheitlichen Kunstmittels beim Klavierspiel*
(Theory of unified art in pianism).[49] At the same time, his wife allegedly published in *Allgemeine Musikzeitung* her protest against Deppe's
"dead-dropping-fingerations and passivity of the body."[50] Probably in

September of 1885 Clark, his wife, and their infant son left for the United States.[51]

Choosing between Chicago, New York, and Boston, they decided to try Boston, speculating that it was the only place where they could "gain a hearing for transcendentalism in any mode."[52] The Clarks settled in Uxbridge, a place that is described in *Iphigenia* as a not very fashionable Boston suburb. In fact, Uxbridge was settled in 1662 and incorporated in 1727, but never as a Bostonian suburb, since it is at least 30 miles southwest of Boston. The Bostonian elite at that time consisted of some four hundred people. Although members of that elite considered themselves as progressive—even avant-garde— Steiniger saw them as quite conservative, devoted to preserving their dominant role in Boston. Steiniger, and probably also Clark, speaking through her mouth, strongly accused the Bostonian society of elitism, corruption, laziness, thriftiness, and decadence. This characterization probably reveals the shocking effect of democracy on the strictly organized, proud, and prudent mind of Prussian-born Steiniger. The couple nevertheless tried to assert their new "Clark-Steiniger" piano-playing method and philosophy.[53] However, following the proverb that nobody is a prophet in one's own country, the Bostonians believed more in orthodox German professors and pianists visiting their country than in native talent. Clark himself remembered a time in his youth when he, quite seriously, followed the opinion widely spread among American artists and public in general in those times: "I was still very much infected by America's national epidemics, according to which Germany is populated only by gods, who are embodied in the form of philosophers."[54]

According to Mathews, the Bostonians liked slightly "detached" persons, but the couple's direct approach, uncompromising spirit, and readiness for sacrifice struck them as eccentric, so much so that they showed reluctance even to help it survive.

Claiming to be "the greatest Beethoven-pianist from Germany ever to come to live in Boston," Anna Steiniger was clearly insulted by the attitude of those people serving to the "hell of fractionality," as she often described American individualism.[55] The Clarks tried to describe the postulates of their new "Clark-Steiniger" method to many people whose opinion weighed a lot in America's public life and art-trend setting. These included Bishop Rivers of the Episcopalian church, Rev. Dr. Peabody, Unitarian rector of Uxbridge University, and even Alcott,[56] who apparently rejected the idea that there could be "any philosophy or education in music at all as high as that in sculpture or painting."[57] They did find some understanding and support from John Sullivan Dwight, a very influential person in Boston's musical life and editor of *Dwight's Journal of Music* (1852-81), and later from W. S. B. Mathews.

Having in general very little success and support, and even having been urged to abandon music and take to teaching French and German to make a living, the couple was forced to suppress their ideas just to ensure their existence. Even when Clark received invitations to demonstrate his method at universities, usually no students were admitted for fear of discussion and commotion.[58] Occasionally, Clark was asked to present lectures such as one on religion of art for the New England Women's Club, or the one on religion of art as a center of education in the salon of an Emily E. J. F. Newhall on the Boston Back Bay. He was regarded as a presenter of the final word in transcendentalism.

Anna Steiniger was not able to bear all the disrespect and abuse manifested toward her and her husband.[59] She died prematurely in January or February of 1891, as a result of several months of rigorous fasting, long mental concentration exercises, and gradual weakening. Clark was forced to continue playing in the traditional manner, to ensure financial support for himself and his three children. In 1892 he published several articles in Mathews's journal *Music*.

The next available evidence of Clark's activity comes only from 1900, when W. S. B. Mathews mentioned a visit to his home in an editorial article of the journal *Music*.[60] By this time Anna Steiniger was deceased for nine years, and Clark (spelled "Clarke" by Mathews) had already remarried—with his sixteen-year-old former American student. This unnamed young lady, described by Mathews as having a beautiful hand and playing with great taste and appreciation, had brought him three more children, in addition to the three left by Steiniger.[61]

Mathews describes in detail the spirit of affection and sympathy in Clark's family. Two of Steiniger's children, a fourteen-year-old girl, who was said to have inherited her mother's countenance, and a ten-year-old boy, were already quite developed as pianists.[62] Clark seemed to have just moved to Chicago, but Mathews mentions that Clark had already lived there (probably right after Anna's death) and then moved to Valparaiso, Indiana, where, at the time the article was published, he still kept his post at a "large normal school,"[63] probably Northern Indiana Normal School, because the announcements show that he played several concerts there. In 1901 Clark was still in the United States, if the date of a letter he received after one of his concerts is to be trusted.[64]

In 1903, however, judging by a review of his concert that appears in an appendix of *Brahms' Noblesse*,[65] he was in Germany again, apparently by invitation from his former student Antonia (Tony) Bandmann and Friedrich Adolf Steinhausen.[66] The "Prime-General-Physician" of the German army supposedly had invited him to Germany in 1903, promising him help in practical realization of his theory. Clark claims that the physician later stole his idea of harmony acquired through spiral motions and tried to exploit it in a book on violin bowing.[67] After that, the same physician, in collaboration with a former student of Clark, published two piano methods.[68] Although he had already encountered plagiarism of his works, Clark was shocked to see the very person who invited him to Berlin behaving in such an unethical manner.[69]

There is no mention of his family from this point on. It is unlikely that Clark, as an ardent Catholic, could just leave his family, or— even less—divorce his wife.[70] Bearing in mind, though, that during the last fourteen years of his life he was on the verge of extreme poverty, it is difficult to imagine how he would be able to support an eight-member family. The circumstances of his return to Europe thus remain so far quite mysterious. It is possible that at this time in his life some events might have occurred in connection with this situation, which gradually turned him into a single-minded, fervor-driven, and relentless seeker of the sole "truth" in art.

This was, nevertheless, by far the most productive period of Clark's life. During the next ten years, Clark—often starving, poor, yet imperturbable in his quest—dedicated his whole being to the idea of total *Harmonie* of the body and the soul: harmony with the universe and with the Creator. He gave concerts, demonstrating his "Cherubim-doctrine"[71] of playing in a standing position, patented his invention of the two-keyboard piano, and worked on founding a university chair for *Harmonie*. However, with little success in America, Clark certainly had even less success with strict, stubborn, and hermetic German institutions. In 1903 he gave five concerts in Berlin prompting, according to him, the works of Bandmann, Steinhausen, and Breithaupt. The first of those concerts took place in Bechstein Hall, where he used the piano in its normal position.[72] For the second one, in Singakademie, he borrowed a piano from a Mr. Duysen and lifted it on wooden blocks.[73] From the end of 1903 he spent twenty-two hungry months in Berlin, followed by eleven months in the same circumstances in Leipzig, where he arrived in October 1905. On 15 August 1907 he made a first attempt of playing at a truly elevated keyboard, lifting the piano onto his writing desk, giving his first concert in this position on 1 or 2 November 1907. In 1909 he played three concerts in Berlin, under the general title of *Pianistenharmonie*. The first of those took place on 22 February, the second on 2 March.[74] He remarked in his journal that he would refrain from further concerts until he could collect enough money to build the special *Harmonie*-piano. On 30 October 1911, in a celebration of Liszt's hundredth birthday, which took place in the Gesangverein in Jena, Clark played Liszt's works on the new piano. There were about sixteen hundred people in the audience, many of which "came with intention to mock and laugh at the *Pianistenharmonie* [but] had to be still, because the large audience was won over with the respect and kindness for the new art and achievement."[75]

In his naiveté, Clark even sent two letters to Emperor Wilhelm II, or at least claimed he did. In the second letter, written on 17 January 1914, already from Zurich, Switzerland, and published in the appendix of *Brahms' Noblesse*,[76] he criticized the emperor for undergoing a health cure. Recommended by royal physicians, the cure consisted of sawing and chopping wood, which the Kaiser executed in the uniform of his hunters.[77] Since Clark objected to any movement that is detached, straight, and disconnected, he reminded the emperor of the words that he himself had said in Fridericianum in Kassel: "We ought to lay the main stress of Education on the Harmonie, which now-a-days is totally lacking in all our philosophy, art, and life."[78]

Professors at the University of Berlin did not accept the notion and any practical use of Clark's concept of *Harmonie*, especially when he asked for a position to teach it. Prof. Kretzschmar, director of the *Hochschule für Musik* in Berlin,[79] stated in 1911 that Clark's *Harmonie* was not of national interest but a private affair. Kretzschmar pointed to Prof. Max Barth's style of playing as an example of the solely acceptable and lawful manner of playing that is supported by the German state.[80] After hearing Barth play under Joachim in the Royal Academy in Berlin, Clark described his static torso, independent finger motions, separated tones, and "petty spelling." Incidentally, Barth was later Wilhelm Kempff's teacher. Obviously feeling deprived and neglected, Clark bitterly remarked in the conclusion of his letter that the third class Order of Red-Eagle bestowed upon a Prof. Hugo Münsterberg, an exchange professor from the United States, was a decoration of "philosophy-assininification."[81] Another Roosevelt exchange professor in Berlin, a professor Sloane, denied financial help to Clark in

January 1913, quoting too many financial obligations toward his family, but nevertheless, according to Clark, possessed the most expensive car on the market, with which he drove to his empty lecture rooms.[82]

It is probable that Clark somehow felt the approach of the war, and immigrated to Switzerland. Soon after he moved, World War I broke out. Clark's movements during the last four years of his life can be reconstructed from various Swiss official documents.[83] Although Clark's residence permit from Höngg claims he arrived from Berlin, with a registration issued by the American authorities there, the certificate of registration from the American consulate in Zurich indicates that he arrived from the United States. If so, Clark must have left Berlin for the United States some time in or after April 1913, because his certificate of registration from Berlin expired on April 21, 1914, and those certificates were renewed annually. Even though the 1915 certificate is missing, the last one, for 1916, with expiration date of April 19, 1917, is on file (see note 2). Continuing with this hypothesis, Clark must have left the United States after only a month or so, traveling this time to Switzerland, where he arrived (or was registered) on June 4, 1913, the day he applied for residence in Höngg, now a part of Zurich. There he stayed at a Mr. A. Dobler's, landlord. He moved to Zurich on March 23, 1914 and stayed at Rothbuchstraße 72, moving on July 8, 1916 to U[ntere?] Hönggerstraße 14, where he stayed with the Vaterlaus family. On October 6, 1916, he moved again, to Hardstraße 1, probably his last residence.

In Zurich, Clark founded his own publishing company, *Pianistenharmoniepresse*, and did not give up his ideal. He continued publishing his journal *Das Musizieren der Zukunft*, which was a continuation of the journal *Music of the Future and of the Present*, published in Chicago from 1901. He was working on, and announced the printing of, books titled *Deppes Ideal: VI Eudämonie Legende* (perhaps a sequel to *Brahms' Noblesse*, which is *V Eudämonie Legende*), *Pianistenharmonie II: Technik*, and *Des Christen Pianistenharmonie*. Leaving several other projects unfinished, Clark died in Zurich on Saturday, 27 January 1917, at 12:20. He was cremated (according to the instructions on his hospital report) on Wednesday, January 31 at 17:30 in Sihlfeld, a then newly built crematorium. His urn was to be deposited in the "next-following" urn-grave, and ironically enough, organ playing at this ceremony was to take place only if "free of charge."

Notes

1. Bettina Walker, *My Musical Experiences* (London: Bentley, 1890; 2nd ed., 1892), 134. Incidentally, she spells his name as "Frederick Steinecke-Clarke."

2. This date is given according to the certificate of registration of American citizen, issued by the consul-general of the United States at Zurich, a Mr. Francis B. Keene, on April 20, 1916, and corroborated by his death certificate, issued by the Kanton hospital in Zurich (which does mention the year 1860, although it is crossed out) and residence control authorities in Zurich. All the other sources indicate 1860 as the year of his birth.

3. The existence of Liebeshain remains to be proven, although it is quite possible that a small unincorporated settlement could have escaped the census at the time: It does not appear either in the 1854 edition of the *New and Complete Gazetteer* or on the 1895 historical atlas of the region. "Three days' walk" could be interpreted as a distance from sixty to ninety miles, which covers the area of the west border of Kane County, De Kalb County, and possibly easternmost areas of either Ogle or Lee counties in Illinois. The above-mentioned certificate of registration states simply "Chicago, Illinois."

4. According to Clark's book *Brahms' Noblesse* (Zurich: Pianisten-harmoniepresse, 1914), the senior Clark was connected with Northwestern Railway—he was apparently a member of the presidium. See Frederic Horace Clark, *Liszts Offenbarung: Schlüssel zur Freiheit des Individuums* (Berlin: C. F. Vieweg, 1907), 14. The description fits the person of Horace Francis Clark (Nov. 29, 1815, Southbury, Conn. – June 19, 1873, New York City). Graduated at Williams College in 1833, he was admitted to the New York bar in 1837, and practiced in that city for twenty years. He was elected as a Democratic representative in the 35th Congress, and as an Independent to the 36th Congress. In 1848 he married a favorite daughter of Commodore Cornelius Vanderbilt. In 1857 he was made a director of the New York & Harlem Railroad, and later became president of the Union Pacific, the Michigan Southern, the Lake Shore, and the Northern Indiana railroads, and director of the New York Central & Hudson River, the Shore Line, the Chicago & Northwestern, and the New Haven, Hartford and Springfield railroads. He was manager of the Western Union Telegraph Company, and president of the Union Trust Company of New York.

Apart from a conspicuous similarity in names and initials to Frederic Horace, and the references Frederic Horace Clark makes to his father's activities, it is difficult to see how this biography of one of the most noted politicians and enterpreneurs of his time could allow for a home built such a long distance from the center of his activities and in such a different spirit (farm life). Perhaps the fact that he stopped practicing law and dedicated himself to railroad construction just a year before Frederic Horace was born is not just a coincidence but, on the other hand, the official records mention that Horace Francis Clark had only one child, Marie Louise, who was married three times and died in 1894. (*The 20th Century Biographical Dictionary of Notable Americans*, Rossiter Johnson, ed. 2: 222 [Boston, Mass.: Biographical Society, 1904]). Also, no mention in any reference to Horace Francis Clark is made of his retreat to the wilderness of Illinois. Clark states that in August 1871 his father experimented with an endless chain on a long elliptical plane which reached far out into Lake Michigan and automatically brought onto shore great buckets of sand. This improved the speed and certainty of sand transportation, otherwise dependent upon boats and weather conditions. Two months later the great fire destroyed Chicago, and because of the winter storms the chain was the only means of delivering the sand for rebuilding the city. With this application he made a fortune, which he invested into the construction of the Central Mississippi Railroad. This account seems quite likely and probable.

Open questions remain as to whether Clark used this person's biography as a fictitious setting for his romantically imbued odyssey, or to what degree his claims might be true. The first references he makes to his life come from Bettina Walker's book, twenty-five years before the next known reference, and in them no mention of his father's activities is made.

5. Although Clark does use the word priest or preacher (*Prediger*), perhaps minister would be more appropriate, because a Catholic priest obviously could not marry. Episcopal priests, however, could marry, but there is no information on the church affiliation here.

6. This is the first of numerous discrepancies encountered in different sources both on and from Clark. According to Clark's *Liszts Offenbarung*, 1, at the age of fourteen he was still in Liebeshain, to where his aunt sent the music. According to Walker's *My Musical Experiences*, 134, and quoted in W. S. B. Mathews's *Music 1* (January 1892): 298, he was already sent to Pittsburgh at the age of twelve, and heard of Liszt for the first time there.

7. Again, this detailed description of his emotional and mental state is to be found only in *Liszts Offenbarung*, where virtually every event in his life has been assigned a connection, and relates to Liszt.

8. *Liszts Offenbarung*, 3.

9. The granduncle, Clark's grandfather's brother, was, according to Clark, a prince, and the son of a prince in Normandy, France. He had reportedly traveled once to Vienna to hear Mozart play. Despite the effect Mozart's playing had on him, the granduncle was allegedly told by Mozart that he did not feel free while playing, and that he could not express his soul completely in his playing. After some political unrest (probably the stormy events of 1789, or even 1848—see below) the granduncle and his brother left everything and fled to Quebec.

The episode involving Mozart does not seem likely, since assuming Clark's granduncle heard Mozart before the political unrests of 1789, and that he was at least ten at that time (would Mozart speak to somebody of that age in those terms?), then in 1872, when the conversation between Frederic Horace and himself apparently took place, he would have been at least 94 years old. Clark does mention his "long beard," probably the result of his old age and the twenty years of hermit-like life in a cave (this last information perhaps makes 1848 the likely exile year).

10. *Liszts Offenbarung*, 15.

11. One of them, a professor from Düsseldorf, is mentioned in both *Liszts Offenbarung* and *Brahms' Noblesse*. This person was instrumental in advising Clark to study for several years at a conservatory prior to any attempt at becoming a Liszt student, and put him on a train to Leipzig (from Rotterdam), according to *Liszts Offenbarung*. In *Brahms' Noblesse*, 19—and only in that book—the same professor introduced him to Brahms (this time in Hamburg).

12. Walker, 136, is the only source according to which Clark actually traveled on foot even from Hamburg, having been left with only a few marks.

13. Louis Maas (1852-1889), a student of Reinecke, taught at the Leipzig Conservatory from 1875-1880, settling afterward in Boston. Ernst Ferdinand Wenzel (1808-1880), a friend of Schumann, taught at the conservatory from its foundation in 1843 (the majority of the English-speaking students were in his class) until his death. Oscar Paul (1836-1898), a student of Plaidy, taught at the conservatory from 1869.

14. Christian Friedrich Kahnt (1823-1897) was the founder of a well-known publishing firm which, from 1857, published Schumann's *Neue Zeitschrift für Musik*.

15. One again encounters a discrepancy here. Walker and, subsequently, Mathews, omit most of these details, found only in *Liszts Offenbarung*, and mention only Clark's escape to Europe from Pittsburgh, via Chicago and New York. According to Walker and Mathews, Clark escaped only because he knew he would not have gotten permission from his parents to sail for Europe.

Furthermore, these sources mention he was actually sent at the age of twelve to "a distant town" (undoubtedly Pittsburgh, Pennsylvania, because he mentions that he lived in the house of a near relation, and that was the town to which his aunt moved after being married. Pittsburgh is also named by Mathews). There he was supposed to learn "the book business" (probably bookkeeping) and first read through some compositions by Liszt.

The experience of playing Liszt's music made him realize that he was not as advanced in his playing as he had thought. It also instilled in him a strong desire to travel to what many considered the center of music teaching at that time—the Leipzig Conservatory. He hoped to develop fully his musical potential there.

Working, giving lessons, and copying music for four years, he saved toward his escape to Hamburg (not Rotterdam, as mentioned in *Liszts Offenbarung*), at the age of sixteen. Having only a few marks in his pocket, he proceeded, according to Walker, to Leipzig on foot. Mathews actually mentions that Clark had fifty dollars for the whole trip from Pittsburgh, spending a fortnight in New York, and winding up with only five dollars in his pocket in Leipzig (*Music* 5, September 1900, 480). After many days without practicing, he played there a polonaise (not the *Chromatic Gallop*, but also interrupted) and sight-read a Mozart sonata. He successfully completed the entrance examination at the Leipzig Conservatory and only then contacted his parents. According to *My Musical Experiences*, he wrote them hoping they would forgive and secure full board for him during the study, and indeed it happened so.

Mathews further mentions Clark's trip from Leipzig to Weimar, Halle, Eisenach, and Switzerland, not mentioning its reason or destination. If it is a reference to Clark's probable journey to Liszt, it is incomplete. It is difficult to think of any other reason for which Clark, impoverished and in a completely foreign environment, would undertake such a journey. According to Mathews, Clark was finally received as a free pupil. In *Brahms' Noblesse* Clark completely neglects to describe circumstances of his arrival in Hamburg.

16. The famous English painter John Ruskin (1819-1900), a champion of the Pre-Raphaelite Brotherhood of painters in the early 1850s, indeed spent substantial time in Italy. Some of his letters from Italy have been edited by Van Akin Burd and published under the title *Christmas Story: John Ruskin's Venetian Letters of 1876-1877* (Newark: University of Delaware Press, 1991) which does confirm he was in Italy at the time (Venice and Milan being relatively close). Clark gives quite a detailed description of the location of Ruskin's apartment "next to the Cathedral . . . in a very narrow street, from which we had a wonderful view of the Cathedral's walls" (*Liszts Offenbarung*, 29). Some elements of Ruskin's biography bear a similarity to Clark's, especially regarding his chastity (Ruskin's marriage was annulled after six years of nonconsummation whereas Clark abstained from sexual relationship during the first several months after marriage, according to a biblical code; both felt themselves frequently alienated from an uncomprehending public, and both regarded human activity as a work of religious devotion applied to natural forms).

17. The only discrepancy here arises regarding his mention of the introductory letter from Kahnt being written in October, while Clark's own calculation of days between Leipzig and Stilfserjoch, where he arrived sometime close to the winter solstice, gives at least ninety days. This means that he either made an error in quoting the date of the letter, or exaggerated his estimate of the traveling time.

18. Liszt was not in Rome in June 1877, but he arrived there in mid-August. Moreover, from Rome he traveled not to Weimar, but to Budapest. If one assumes that this kind of factual error is accidental, it would be relatively easy to justify by noting that the events mentioned took place thirty years before they were actually described in *Liszts Offenbarung*. He confirms the year, though, in several instances, such as his journal *Das Musizieren der Zukunft* Vol. 1 No. IV (December 1907), 231.

19. This information is corroborated in *Brahms' Noblesse*, in which Clark even adds the house-number "13." A curious fact worthy of mention is Clark's claim that while in Leipzig he heard Brahms perform his first piano concerto for the first time. This event actually ends *Brahms' Noblesse*, but is

in itself absolutely untrue and impossible, since the first performance of this concerto, with the composer as the soloist and Joachim conducting, took place on January 22, 1859, in Hannover. The first performance in Leipzig took place only five days later, followed by the March 24 performance in Hamburg. At the time Clark was one month old and therefore his explicit wording is difficult to explain: "In these concerts [in Gewandhaus], I heard Brahms play his first concerto for the first time in public." (*Brahms' Noblesse*, 397) It is true, though, that Brahms played in Leipzig in January 1877—Clark might have misunderstood the occasion or remembered it incorrectly. One possible explanation would be that the syntax of his English got progressively influenced by that of the German language, and therefore this construction might be a clumsy way of saying that this was the first time he (Clark) heard Brahms perform this concerto (implying there was at least one more subsequent occasion, which is not improbable). On the other hand, his formulation in German, found in *Das Musizieren der Zukunft* Vol. 2 No. 1 (March 1912), 345, is quite explicit, insisting again on the incorrect year and on the fact that it was the first performance ever. After the concert, Clark heard very critical remarks on Brahms's playing from Salomon Jadassohn, and even his own teacher, Dr. Oscar Paul. The latter announced to him that in a week Hans von Bülow would be playing there, and "he can play on the piano."

20. According to *Das Musizieren der Zukunft* Vol. 2 No. 1 (August 1912): 373, his first teaching position was at the Detroit Conservatory of Music.

21. Ludwig Deppe (1828-1890) was conductor of a choral society in Hamburg and was educated as a violinist by a student of Ludwig Spohr. Apparently it was due to him that the famous Russian pianist and pedagogue (student of Leschetizky, teacher of Prokofiev) Anna Essipoff (1851-1914) made her first German appearance. Although he appears not to have had any professional training as a pianist, he became very well known as a piano teacher.

22. According to *Das Musizieren der Zukunft* Vol. 2 No. 1 (March 1912).

23. This is corroborated by his mention of a "prospectus" on piano playing, allegedly written in the United States in 1880. This seems to be his first written work (not found).

24. Spelled "Herrlick" and "Herrlich" in F. H. Clark's *Iphigenia, Baroness of Styne* (London: Pure Music Society, priv. ed., 1896), this was probably Heinrich Ehrlich, Austrian pianist (1822-1899), a pupil of Henselt and Thalberg, who lived in Hannover and Berlin. He taught at the Stern Conservatory in Berlin from 1864 to 1872 and from 1886 to 1898, but not at the time when Clark met him, and was a proponent of Paul's approach.

25. In *Liszts Offenbarung* Clark uses the German name for Tartu: Dorpat. It seems that this unnamed baroness through whom, as he claimed in *Liszts Offenbarung*, he also sent a copy of his own etudes to Liszt, was actually Countess de Matuschka (see note 38). She was married to the Baron de Rosenberg (a step down in rank, but the Rosenbergs were apparently a branch of the famous English Coutts family). Her name is not given in *Iphigenia*, ex-

cept that she married "Baron von Tese, near Riga, in Livonia" (Livonia being the name feudal German conquerors gave to the area nowadays belonging to Latvia). There it is also stated that she was an intimate friend of Princess Bismarck, and that she saw Clark going to the Berlin Palace of the Royal Chancellor. Her friend Gisela von Arnim tried to arrange a meeting with Clark, asking Deppe for piano lessons and probably hoping she would see Clark there. When Deppe lost his nerve with the Baroness (and a very shattering characterization of the noblemen's state of mind and concentration is given by Clark) he handed her over to Anna Steiniger, his assistant and Clark's future wife. After the Baroness's return from Africa, the Clarks were already married, and she invited them to her estate in Riga, Inzeem, Quellenhof. They went there in 1883 and stayed for four months. Through her they met a "Princess Maiendorf," who was by marriage a baroness, and kept a long-term friendship with Liszt. When her husband died, she moved to Weimar and lived there at least until Liszt's death. This information is correct, as corroborated by Klára Hamburger in her book *Liszt* (Budapest: Corvina, 1987), 165. There Olga von Meyendorff, née princess Gorchakova, is described as the young widow of the Russian envoy formerly in Rome and reassigned to Weimar. Apparently she was a very arrogant woman of great erudition who used to scrutinize severely every one of Liszt's female students, occasionally causing some embarrassing scenes. According to Princess Wittgenstein, there might have been more than a friendship between the two.

26. These two events have been placed in *Liszts Offenbarung* at the time before he met Anna, although in *Iphigenia* all Russian episodes happen after their marriage.

27. *Music* 5 (September 1900): 480, by W. S. B. Mathews. He further stated that Clark was one of the original discoverers of Deppe, switching to him from Kullak. Fay's dispute appeared in the October issue.

28. Amy Fay, *Music Study in Germany* (Chicago: Jansen, McClurg, 1880).

29. Clark, however, had a different opinion about this incident in his *Liszts Offenbarung*, 243:

> During my last visit to Chicago, a former female student of Liszt and Deppe tried to talk me into taking lessons from Deppe instead of Dr. Paul when I return to Germany. I resisted the idea, because everything that I have heard of Deppe and his wild idea of weight-playing was unattractive to me. When I was already on my way to New York, this lady sent me a book, asking me to forward it to Deppe, which I did. On that occasion Deppe invited me to hear his student Anna Steiniger play a piano concerto. I was momentarily fascinated with her. It was love at first sight, and she soon became my wife.

(Bei meinem letzten Besuch in Chicago hatte mich eine Schülerin Liszts und Deppes einzureden gesucht, ich solle bei Deppe anstatt bei Dr. Paul bei meiner Rückkehr nach Deutschland Unterricht nehmen. Ich sträubte mich dagegen, weil alles, was ich über Deppe gelesen hatte, wegen seiner mir töricht erscheinenden "Idee" des "Gewichtspiels" mir Abneigung eingeflößt hatte. Als ich nach New York schon unterwegs war, schickte mir diese Dame ein Buch mit der Bitte, ich möchte es Deppe in Berlin überbringen. Ich tat das denn auch, und Deppe forderte mich auf, von seiner Schülerin Anna Steiniger ein Klavierkonzert spielen zu hören. Ich war sofort fasziniert von der Spielerin. Es war Liebe auf den ersten Blick, und bald war sie meine Frau.)

For more on the relationship between Fay and Clark, see chapter 9.

30. John Storer Cobb, *Anna Steiniger, a Biographical Sketch: In Which Is Contained a Suggestion of the Clark-Steiniger System of Piano-forte Playing* (Boston: Schirmer, 1886), 21.

31. Cobb (or rather, the Clarks, since they compiled the information for him) states that Clark met Deppe accidentally, and then heard Anna at one of her customary soirées.

32. *Iphigenia*, 130.

33. *Iphigenia*, 134.

34. According to *Das Musizieren der Zukunft* Vol. 1 No. 4 (January 1909), 311, apparently both Moszkowski and Liszt, in conversations with Clark, qualified Deppe as a "Klavierschwindler" ("piano-swindler").

35. By 1913, at the latest, he must have possessed some official document that served as a basis for his U. S. Certificate of Registration in Germany.

36. This incident, in a slightly different form, is reported also by Carl Lachmund in his book *Mein Leben mit Franz Liszt* (My life with Franz Liszt). See Bertrand Ott, *Liszt et la pedagogie du piano* (Issy-les-Moulineaux: Editions scientifiques et psychologiques, 1978), 50-51. Although it is missing in the English translation of the book, it appears in Alan Walker's *Living with Liszt: From the Diary of Carl Lachmund, an American Pupil of Liszt, 1882-1884*, ed. Alan Walker (Stuyvesant, N.Y.: Pendragon, 1995), 252-254. This is one of the rare events which can actually be cross-checked. According to Lachmund, who himself learned about it from Liszt, Clark and his wife arrived in Weimar and wanted to play for Liszt. As Liszt was already tired from his own work he declined this, and also refused to answer any of the questions Clark had. They parted in bad spirits. Liszt then asked Lachmund to convey to Clark, if he met him, that he would have kind words for him if they met again. From this it is not clear if Clark and Liszt had met before, but the reconciliatory spirit of Liszt (who probably overreacted some-

what during the meeting) certainly leaves open the possibility of their meeting at some later time.

37. According to *Iphigenia* it was through Olga von Meyendorff that Clark sent a copy of several of his concert etudes to Liszt. The etudes with double 3rds, 4ths, 6ths, and octaves Liszt apparently deemed among the most difficult things ever written and, according to Clark, "with ideas of real geniality." In *Iphigenia* Liszt also never finds out the name of the author.

38. Whereas in *Liszts Offenbarung* Clark does not mention his wife at all when describing Countess de Matuschka and the events in Russia, Cobb similarly does not mention Clark when recounting Steiniger's successes and friendships there. It is very likely that Matuschka and Tiesenhauser-Manteuffel, who was spelled "Tiesenhausen" in Clark's preface to the *Three Impromptus* op. 7 (1884), are one and the same person. Cobb states that Matuschka, apparently a connoisseur in arts, liked Steiniger's playing very much and arranged the presence of Carl Reinecke at her concert during the sixth Silesian Music Festival. Reinecke invited Steiniger for the next season (1884) to the Gewandhaus in Leipzig. In Livonia, Steiniger appeared at the invitation of Baroness Tiesenhauser-Manteuffel, who had an estate in Riga. Steiniger was heard there by the Land Marshall, Baron von Bock, the third husband (married in 1850) of Wilhelmine Schröder-Devrient (1804-1860), celebrated German soprano who sang Leonore in *Fidelio* in the presence of Beethoven and Agathe in *Der Freischütz* under Weber (both in 1822).

39. Bettina von Arnim, née Brentano, whom Beethoven had met in 1810, married one of her brother's friends, Achim von Arnim, who was a poet and novelist. Beethoven's correspondence with her is often cited in his biographies.

40. *Iphigenia*, 196.

41. Undoubtedly it is Franz Reuleaux (1829-1905), whose *Lehrbuch der Kinematik*, 2 vols. (Braunschweig: Vieweg, 1875-1900), Clark must have studied. The first volume, *Theoretical Kinematics*, was translated in London by Alex B. W. Kennedy and published in 1876 by Macmillan.

42. *Liszts Offenbarung*, 272.

43. *Iphigenia*, 227; *Brahms' Noblesse*, 411. Although a sensation of a "divine revelation" could be easily accounted for, in a person of such fervent religious disposition, it is more likely just a graphic description of the moment when all of the elements of his theory, which were in his mind for quite a while, came together.

44. The germ of the new idea actually reaches far back, all the way to Clark's childhood. See description in chapter 4.

45. *Eutonie* is the term she used to describe equal tension, as a reaction to Deppe's "free finger fall" theory. Steiniger insisted there there is only a "controlled finger fall," which is true.

46. According to Clark, Deppe's article was published three times: first as a private edition, then in *Deutsche Musiker Zeitung,* 11 July 1885, and finally as a brochure in 1886 by Heroldsche Buchhandlung. According to *The*

New Grove Dictionary of Music and Musicians (1980), s.v. "Deppe, Ludwig" it was published also in *Der Klavierlehrer*, vii, 1885).

47. Perhaps during that trip he also traveled to the lake resort Warnemünde, as described in *Das Musizieren*, Vol. 2 No. 1 (August 1912): 370, to deliver Anna's manuscript—a reaction to Deppe's claims—to Otto Lessmann, editor of *Allgemeine Musikzeitung*.

48. Rudolf Christoph Eucken (1846-1926) was a German philosopher who taught in Basel and from 1874 in Jena. He was an idealist philosopher who developed a flexible system over a period of several decades. In 1908 he was awarded the Nobel Prize for Literature "in recognition of his earnest search for truth, his penetrating power of thought, his wide range of vision, and the warmth and strength in presentation with which in his numerous works he has vindicated and developed an idealistic philosophy of life."

Eucken apparently recommended to Clark that he speak with Westphal who "writes now works based on this principle of the proportionality of freedom in time of the harmonious classicism, of which you spoke." (*Liszts Offenbarung*, 297).

Indeed, Rudolf Georg Hermann Westphal (1826-1892) published several works related to metrical aspects of music and language: in 1865 he published *Geschichte der alten und mittelalterlichen Musik* and *System der antiken Rhythmik* (Breslau, F. E. C. Leuckart), in 1866 *Scriptores metrici graeci* (Leipzig, B. G. Teubner), in 1869 *Philosophisch-historische Grammatik der deutschen Sprache* (Jena, Mauke), in 1870 *Theorie der neuhochdeutschen Metrik* (Jena, C. Doebereiner), in 1872 *Elemente des musikalischen Rhythmus mit besonderer Rücksicht auf unsere Opern-musik* (Jena, H. Costenoble), in 1880 *Allgemeine Theorie der musikalischen Rhythmik seit J. S. Bach* (Leipzig, Breitkopf & Härtel), and in 1883 *Die musik des griechischen Alterthumes* (Leipzig, Veit).

49. Berlin: Raabe & Plothow, 1885.

50. *Brahms' Noblesse*, 249. Confirmed in *Das Musizieren*, Vol. 2 No. 1, August 1912. The article was published on 28 August 1885 in *Allgemeine Musikzeitung*.

51. Although the first born baby was a son (according to *Iphigenia*, 223, and the journal *Das Musizieren der Zukunft* Vol. 1 No. 4 [December 1907], 259), Mathews mentions a fourteen-year-old girl as the "oldest daughter" in the family in 1900 (*Music* 5 [September 1900]: 481). It is impossible to deduct whether this infers that she was the oldest of the daughters in the family or the oldest child. This would be a contradiction, since it is certain that the Clarks did not have children for three years after the marriage, and that the first one, born after October 1886 (probably early 1887) seems to be the daughter Mathews refers to. Possibly, Anna Steiniger (or Clark) deliberately changed the fact, as was apparently done with many of the names in *Iphigenia*. This would have been, presumably, to protect certain individuals or avoid conflicts with those who were alive at the time of printing. However, according to *Iphigenia*, the first child was born while the family was still in

Germany, while in the same book it is stated that for the first three years of their marriage they had no children. Since the marriage took place in 1882, as confirmed in Mathews's *A Hundred Years of Music in America* (G. L. Howe: 1889), s.v. "Clark, Anna Steiniger," hypothetically the first child could have been a son born in 1885, who then must have had died in his early infancy—certainly prior to 1900 when Mathews saw the family. The girl he mentions as the oldest could thus have been born in 1886 as the oldest surviving child. However, there is a son mentioned as the "person to be informed in case of death or accident," on the certificate of registration of American citizen of 1916, issued in Zurich: a Fritz S. Clark, "c/o Union Bank Note Co., Kansas City, Missouri."

52. *Iphigenia*, 290. Chicago was described to them as "composed mostly of butchers, anarchists, mindless beer-brewers, and outlawed peasants"—not a bright perspective for the couple.

53. According to *A Hundred Years of Music in America,* ed. W. S. B. Mathews (Chicago: G. L. Howe, 1889) s.v. "Clark, Anna Steiniger," they had a music school in Cambridge, Massachusetts.

54. *Das Musizieren* Vol. 2 No. 1 (August 1912): 366.

55. *Iphigenia*, 316.

56. Presumably Amos Bronson Alcott (1799-1888).

57. *Iphigenia*, 301.

58. A letter to this effect from Boston University is mentioned in *Iphigenia*, 355. The episode is corroborated by the preface of *The Artists Unified* (Chicago: Pure Music Society, 1895), Clark's edition of piano pieces. Clark writes: "In 1885 the New England Conservatory sent me in Boston an official statement that the faculty would gladly hear a lecture on this matter, but the students could not be allowed to do so because it would doubtless cause in their minds great questioning of their present methods!" A further mention of this incident comes from the journal *Music of the Future and of the Present* Vol. 1 No. 3 (December 1901), 11. According to Clark, in 1886 Carl Faelten (who he spells "Faelton," or "Failtown," in *Iphigenia*), the director of the New England Conservatory in Boston, dined at Clarks' Cambridge [*sic!* not Uxbridge] home and remarked: "I do not dare to let your husband lecture before the Conservatory because knowledge of the truth of harmonious activity in pianism would so set the students to thinking and questioning the present methods of percussion and disconnecting that it would be bad for them." Faelten (1846-1925) was director from 1890-1897 and at 1886 was only a professor at the conservatory. In 1897 together with his brother Reinhold he founded the Faelten Pianoforte School in Boston.

59. See chapter 2.

60. *Music* 5 (September 1900): 480-82.

61. This is corroborated by the hospital death certificate, where in handwriting along a margin one can read in German: "6 children in America." No other information concerning Clark's second wife has come to light.

62. Apparently the third child from his marriage to Steiniger was also a girl.

63. *Music* 5, 482.

64. A. C. Klein, director of the Dubuque Academy of Music, wrote a letter on 28 October 1901, which is quoted in *Music of the Future and of the Present*, Vol. 1 No. 3 (December 1901), 14: "I trust you will be very careful of your health and not waste your efforts on the undeserving. . . . Your playing was so dignified, so noble and uplifting that I love to recall it, in fact I have been filled with it ever since." Klein was apparently a student of Kullak and married a pianist educated by Friedrich Wieck.

65. *Brahms' Noblesse*, 434-35.

66. Steinhausen was at the time medical officer in the German Army, with a high rank *(Oberstabsarzt)*—Clark calls him "Prime-General-Physician."

67. Clark mentions only the publisher and the date: Breitkopf und Härtel, 1903. The work in question was *Die Physiologie der Bogenführung* (Physiology of bowing) (Leipzig: Breitkopf und Härtel, 1903).

68. Clark again gives only Breitkopf & Härtel, 1905, 1907. Friedrich Adolf Steinhausen wrote *Über die physiologischen Fehler und die Umgestaltung der Klavier-Technik* (On the physiological errors and the rearrangement of piano technique) (Leipzig: Breitkopf & Härtel, 1905). It is not certain if Clark was thinking of a completely different work, or of later editions of the same work, the third edition of which was published in 1913, in a revision by L. Riemann Essen. The student Clark mentions is almost certainly Antonia (Tony) Bandmann, whom he calls "Steinhausen's friend."

69. Clark asserts that Elisabeth Caland stole his ideas and introduced them as her own, interspersing them with those coming from Ludwig Deppe, the person about whom she was actually writing. The relationship between Clark and his environment deserves a special comment, and is the subject of chapter 9. Elisabeth Caland wrote *Die Deppesche Lehre des Klavierspiels* (Stuttgart: Ebner, 1897; 4th ed., 1912), and *Technische Ratschläge für Klavierspieler* (Stuttgart: Ebner, 1912). Describing Caland's work, Rudolf M. Breithaupt, in the third edition of his book *Die natürliche Klaviertechnik* (Leipzig: C. F. Kahnt Nachfolger, 1912; 1st ed. 1905), and only in that edition, recognizes Clark as the person who first introduced those ideas in Clark's *Die Lehre des einheitlichen Kunstmittels beim Klavierspiel* (Berlin: Raabe & Plotow, 1885). See chapter 5.

In an appendix on schools and methods in the same book, next to the title of Clark's *Die Lehre*, Breithaupt remarks: "The oldest scientific explanation (basis) of the modern psycho-physiological method" (*Die natürliche Klaviertechnik*, 771).

Steinhausen himself did pay his tribute to Clark's pioneer efforts. In his work *Die physiologischen Fehler*, 5, he states that "F. Clark-Steiniger, a student of Deppe, can be given the credit and the merit of a first scientific attempt (of applying physiologically-based movements in the performing art)."

70. It seems beyond doubt that Clark did indeed have six children. The silence about them and about his second marriage is hard to understand. The report from the Kanton hospital in Zurich states: "divorced from?" the certificate of registration has the whole section crossed out, although it mentions his son. This lack of accuracy has unfortunately deprived us of related information. The registration from Höngg has, however: "Zivilstand: verw.[itwet] alleinst.[ehend]" (Marital status: widower, solitary). The registration from Zurich declares him divorced, but the official death certificate, original as well as a 1997 reissue, explains that at the time of his death his marital status was not proven, and therefore declares it as "unknown."

71. See chapter 4.

72. He received a letter from Mr. Bechstein saying that he has to use the instrument "as is" because the previous night it was used by Mr. Reisenauer (Alfred Reisenauer, a student of Liszt) who played at normal height and with a normal chair and praised the piano.

73. These blocks were about 5 inches high and were supposedly earlier always used by Raif, his former teacher. Clark mentions on several occasions that Raif was the only pianist of some standing who agreed with Clark's ideas. More on the development of this idea in chapter 6.

74. No date is given for the third one.

75. *Das Musizieren*, Vol. 2 No. 1 (March 1912), 341.

76. *Brahms' Noblesse*, 404-33.

77. This letter was written as a reaction to the article "Kaiser Wilhelm sägt Holz," *Tages-Anzeiger* (Zürich), 14 January 1914, as quoted in Clark, *Brahms' Noblesse*, 404. However, as Alan Walker points out in his *Living with Liszt: From the Diary of Carl Lachmund, an American Pupil of Liszt, 1882-1884*, ed. Alan Walker (Stuyvesant, N.Y.: Pendragon, 1995), 254, this was a serious error, since the emperor had a withered arm, and whatever movements he was applying were the only ones he was capable of executing.

78. *Brahms' Noblesse*, 405. This apparently happened on 19 August 1911. When Clark sent a letter of thanks for these words to His Majesty (this is probably the first of the two letters mentioned), he got the reply from the minister of culture stating that "the German government makes no provision for the *Harmonie*." When calling upon the Kaiser's words, Clark was similarly rejected by other important individuals, such as Erich Schmidt, rector of the University of Berlin, who said that he could not talk about the *Harmonie* because he did not know anything about it.

79. *Brahms' Noblesse*, 421. The Professor Kretzschmar (spelled "Kretschmar" by Clark) referred to was undoubtedly August Ferdinand Hermann Kretzschmar (1848-1924), professor at the University of Berlin from 1904, and in 1909-20 also the director of the Hochschule für Musik there.

80. See *Brahms' Noblesse*, 224.

81. Münsterberg (1863-1916) was a Harvard professor of psychology (see *Dictionary of American Biography*). In 1910 he was appointed exchange professor from Harvard to the University of Berlin. Ironically, one of his basic

beliefs was that only the fostering of cultural ties between the two nations could bring about harmony among them. Devoting therefore much of his time in Berlin to the creation of the America Institute, he apparently did not apply his notion of "harmony" on an individual level. Clark sent him the 1908 numbers of his journal *Das Musizieren der Zukunft* but was criticized for lifting the keyboard to shoulder level, which, in Münsterberg's eyes, was an act of a charlatan. According to Clark, Münsterberg stated that "the soul has nothing to do with the body, because he follows Kant and Plato in philosophy," (*Brahms' Noblesse*, 425), and claimed that he would have otherwise helped Clark.

82. *Brahms' Noblesse*, 427.

83. For these I am indebted to Prof. Christian Spring.

2

Anna Steiniger's Life and Education

Anna Steiniger was a prominent German (Prussian) pianist. She had given many concerts throughout Europe and Russia before coming to the United States, and was included in *A Hundred Years of Music in America* (1889), a musical dictionary edited by W. S. B. Mathews.[1] The most important sources regarding her biography are Frederic Horace Clark's *Iphigenia, Baroness of Styne*,[2] and John Storer Cobb's *Anna Steiniger, a Biographical Sketch: In Which Is Contained a Suggestion of the Clark-Steiniger System of Piano-Forte Playing.*[3] She is also mentioned in some detail in Bettina Walker's *My Musical Experiences.*[4] The first three sources are very similar regarding her life. Mathews was apparently a fairly good friend of the Clark family, mentioning the Clarks on several occasions in his journal *Music.* Regarding *Iphigenia* Clark himself claimed that he received Anna Steiniger's biographical papers six years after she was deceased, and was asked to arrange them for publication. In the foreword, Clark presented himself as a third person and a student of both Clarks, claiming he had been under the tutelage of those two philosophical musicians longer than any other American. He was obviously trying to give the impression of an impartial and objective scholar, and even went so far as to claim that her husband had "departed from this life in the grief consequent upon her death."[5] This was to be his "work of love" for his great music teacher. In the whole work (460 pages), most of the historical personages are given pseudonyms, which are fairly easy to decipher (styne = Stein = Steiniger). The book received some praise, notably from Charles Warren Stoddard, professor of literature at the universities of California and Washington, D.C., and in *Revista Musical Italiana*.[6]

As regards Cobb's book, its main failure was revealed by Anna Steiniger (or Clark himself) in *Iphigenia*. Clark had been asked by "some friends" (Cobb) to write out some notes for a biography of Anna. In doing so, the couple unconsciously asserted that she had already realized Clark's ideas in her playing—which never really happened—and also, to reinforce that statement, those same "friends" placed the events so that her last great European successes were made to come after she was supposed to have realized Clark's teachings. The deception was unintentional and easy to detect for the public at her concerts, because everybody could see that she made independent movements without any harmonically related motions. Without the cross-reference, though, it would not have been noticed today.[7]

Anna Steiniger[8] seems to have been born on April 19 of the stormy year 1848 in Magdeburg.[9] Her grandfather was apparently a baron in Vienna. Whether Steiniger really was a baroness or not is impossible to determine. Clark might have been referring to the title as inherited from her grandfather. After participating in a rebellion against the Austrian government, he fled the country and entered the Prussian army as a commoner. Herr Styne (Stein), as he called himself now, married a common woman from Stettin, and died a year later while serving under Frederick the Great. The wife died the following year, leaving one child: Anna's father, whose name is never mentioned.

The father was raised in a military orphan asylum, and became a captain in the Prussian army and also an instructor in the Royal Artillery School. He married one of many daughters of a Lutheran preacher from a village near Magdeburg. The first born child in the family was a daughter, Julia, followed by sons Maximilian and Fritz. Anna was the fourth and last child, therefore very close to her father who taught her how to love "whether or not love be requited."[10] For her older brother Fritz, though, she felt an almost unnaturally intense love. Neither of the parents was interested in music. The father even forbade it, because artistic principles at such an age would have soon conflicted with the Prussian pedagogical spirit. With Prussians, according to her own words, love for church was displaced with love for the army. Nevertheless, Anna wanted to play piano from the age of five.

When she was seven, the family moved to Berlin, where her father was put in charge of the Royal Artillery Academy.[11] Just before they moved, her older brother Maximilian died from a fall, which had resulted in a two-year-long spine disease.[12] After two years, when Anna was nine, her father died from a digestive system collapse. This was almost certainly a consequence of his rigorous lifestyle, habits, and duties. Left with a small pension, the family found itself in financial difficulties. Fritz joined the army, and Julia became a teacher.[13] A few weeks after Herr Steiniger's burial, a piano was purchased for Anna. Her future work as a piano teacher was to secure further financial support for the family. From the very beginning of her studies, Anna determined to be a refutation of the Prussian assertion that "musicians are generally no more intelligent than 'cows.'"[14]

She started teaching piano during her second year of study. Before the end of the same year she played a Mozart concerto for the Military Social Club. At the age of ten, she started playing regularly for audiences almost every month, including pieces like Chopin's first Scherzo and E-minor concerto (!). She accompanied for the *Singakademie*, and its director Edward Grell became her mentor.[15] He directed her towards Agthe, who was also Theodore Kullak's teacher.[16] Before she turned eighteen, Anna was entirely self-supporting. She spent two years with Agthe, who was already old and senile. He gave her tasks such as repeating a hundred times the last three measures of Czerny's Etude no. 12 in F major, in the speed indicated by Czerny, while he dozed off.[17] Even so, at that time she performed on three occasions for the philharmonic concerts given in the Barbarini Palace in Potsdam, playing, among other pieces, Beethoven's Concerto No. 5.

Be it as it may, Agthe was nevertheless more conscientious, intense, and gradual in his approach than a Prof. Gross, with whom Steiniger also tried studying. He was less known and forced her to play too difficult pieces in too fast tempos, apparently being satisfied with superficiality in technique and expression. His approach disregarded a scientific, or at least organized, approach to technique.[18] Due to a nervous strain, caused by such changes, Steiniger's health deteriorated and she spent the spring and summer, presumably of 1868, recuperating in the Harz Mountains. During 1868 and 1869 she studied with Theodore Kullak, who apparently represented a unification of the characteristics of her two past teachers.[19]

Her brother Fritz contracted consumption during the siege of Paris[20] and died from it in Anna's arms in 1871. After this tremendous shock, she became intent on a search for the true principles of piano playing, and at about this time she met Ludwig Deppe.[21]

Although Deppe apparently had no professional training as a pianist, his approach to piano playing attracted many students and Anna was no exception. She became his student and stayed with him, it seems, for twelve years, despite the fact that Clark and Steiniger often both describe him as a conceited male chauvinist.[22] In a year he allowed her to take students herself, and she virtually became his assistant. After almost two years of analyzing Deppe's method, Steiniger realized that his artistic intuition was not backed up by equal knowledge of physiology. Cobb explains that at this moment she started to understand the role of the shoulder in playing as the region in which lies the source for the application of power, and the shoulder joint, as the center of motion for lateral action.[23] This was then the involuntary deceit disclosed in *Iphigenia*, because these events were placed in the biography before she met Clark, who was most certainly the person to make her realize the role of the shoulder.[24]

Steiniger played publicly quite a lot at the time, and was associated with such musicians as Etelka Gerster, Aafke Kuypers, and Anna Schimon-Regan, all well-known singers.[25] She was invited twice to London to teach students who were followers of Deppe's piano school.[26] Probably in the summer of 1879 she was invited by the Austrian prince of Reuss[27] to his palace at Ernstbrunn, near Vienna. She was to teach his two daughters and a 22-year-old prince. Refusing to accept courtly flattery, hypocrisy, and formal etiquette, she fled back to Berlin in midsummer. A crisis, brought about when she realized that she was not on the right path while following Deppe's advice, combined with a return of her mother's serious illness, forced her to forgo all engagements for the next two or three years. In the winter of 1882-83 she appeared again in a tour around Germany, accompanying a singer.[28] The aforementioned Countess de Matuschka talked Carl Reinecke[29] into coming and listening to Steiniger's recital at the sixth Silesian Music Festival,[30] and invited her to give a concert in the Leipzig Gewandhaus in the next season. After her great success there, she played in Berlin, Magdeburg, and also in Riga. After her return to Germany, she played only once again: her European farewell concert took place in Düsseldorf, where the program included her favorite *Tageszeiten* by Joachim Raff and Beethoven's *Eroica* variations.

In the United States, her official debut seems to have been the fifth season concert of the Boston Symphony Orchestra in Boston Music Hall, where on 14 November 1885 she played Beethoven's Fourth Concerto under the baton of Johann Gayritey.[31] Purity, refinement, intelligence, warmth, and perfect *cantabile* were the words most often used in reviews of this concert. After this, Mr. Gericke-Gayritey engaged her as piano soloist with the Boston Symphony Orchestra during its western tour in April 1886, when she played in Cincinnati, Chicago, Cleveland, and other cities.[32] Developing quite an active career, Steiniger played, according to Cobb, five seasons of recitals covering major pieces written for the piano, including chamber works, and at the same time four seasons of recitals dedicated exclusively to the piano music of Beethoven. Thus, in January and February of 1886 she gave a series of six Beethoven concerts in Chickering Hall, Boston. During the first of the five piano music seasons she was assisted by the concertmaster of the orchestra, a Mr. Crysdale,[33] during the second by Crysdale and Clark, the third only by Clark, while for the last two she played alone. During the last two years she began taking small loans from aristocratic ladies, and arranged to receive fifty dollars monthly for a year from a committee, to withdraw with Clark to a retreat.

Anna Steiniger's nerves were not strong enough for the degradation and general boycott the two of them suffered because of their insistance on their new piano method. She made her last concert appearance (Schumann's concerto) with the Boston Symphony Orchestra conducted by a Mr. Ishknic (?) in the Boston Music Hall.[34] After spending five years in Boston, in early May 1890 they retreated to a lone farmhouse at the foot of Mt. Desert: a rest she had long looked forward to. There she accepted the advice from a Dr. Charles Dickens (another pseudonym?), Clark's acquaintance and a person with strong ties to the Christian Science and Californian Kaweah Colony teachings,[35] and decided to spend five hours daily in meditation, helped by fasting. She hoped to attain higher spheres of conscience and self-awareness. In that condition, she saw (influenced by a network of Clark's friends) that she should sacrifice herself to free her husband's genius. One can assume that under the conditions she lost her judgment and either ran out into a raging snowstorm, as dramatically described in *Iphigenia*, or probably just induced her own death by losing the will to continue living, a result of the strict meditation and fasting procedures. She died, apparently in late January or early February of 1891,[36] seemingly without revealing the location of her diary (or, better, reflections), which she had written during the last month of her life.[37]

Notes

1. W. S. B. Mathews, ed., *A Hundred Years of Music in America* (Chicago: G. L. Howe, 1889), s.v. "Clark-Steiniger, Anna."

2. *Iphigenia, Baroness of Styne: a Story of the "Divine Impatience," an Approximate Autobiography* (London: Pure Music Society, priv. ed., 1896).

3. *Anna Steiniger, a Biographical Sketch: In Which Is Contained a Suggestion of the Clark-Steiniger System of Piano-forte Playing* (Boston: Schirmer, 1886). Cobb seems to have been an expert on cremation (*A Quartercentury of Cremation in North America* [Boston, Knight and Millet, 1901]), and also published translations of the *Nibelungenlied* and some of Goethe's poems. In addition, there is the *History of Hunstanton, Norfolk: with which is incorporated a narrative of the life of St. Edmund, king and martyr (9. Century)* (London: Jarrold, 1868). He was also the editor during the second year of the two-year existence of *The Nationalist,* a radical Nationalist Educational Association journal.

4. London: Bentley, 1890.

5. *Iphigenia,* i.

6. Stoddard writes:

> I have not had another such spiritual revival in all these years— now thirty or more. . . . never was a woman's heart laid more completely bare. . . . I congratulate Mr. Clark on having given us a most noble book; one which should profoundly influence all who are capable of appreciating it. . . . I wish all musicians might possess it." (As quoted in *Music of the Future and of the Present,* Vol. 1 No. 3 [December 1901], back cover [?])

The following review appeared in *Revista Musical Italiana,* 3rd year, No. 4 Turin, (April 1897), as quoted in the same place:

> It is difficult to give an efficient idea of Clark's method or technique which is surely superior to the present schools. . . . I admire Clark's book because it is the work of an enthusiastic artist, of an intelligent critic, and of a good-hearted man. He deserves such readers as they who know how to study his cultivated mind and his choice musical talent until they can comprehend.

7. *Iphigenia,* 363.

8. "Anna Clark-Steininger," according to Kurt Johnen in *Musik in der Geschichte und Gegenwart,* s.v. "Deppe, Ludwig."

9. Cobb and Howe cite Magdeburg, whereas in *Iphigenia* Potsdam is given as her birthplace. Furthermore, she (or Clark) mentions that her family

lived near the rear of the old Potsdam cathedral, where she played under its flying butresses.

10. *Iphigenia*, 2.

11. In Cobb, 4: Royal Artillery Bureau.

12. Maximilian is completely omitted in Cobb.

13. Julia then spent several years in "Wiesdeden," probably Wiesbaden, and by the 1880s moved to Romania, where she was a tutor ("preceptress") in the royal family.

14. *Iphigenia*, 15.

15. Edward Grell (1800-1886) became a member of the *Singakademie* at the age of 17 and remained connected with it until his death, directing it from 1853 to 1876.

16. "Agthe" according to Cobb. Albrecht Wilhelm Johann Agthe (1790-1873) was active as a pianist, teacher, and composer. In *Iphigenia* Agthe and Kullak are mentioned as "Aggatz" and "Calluc."

17. Cobb mentions that she took her first lesson from Agthe as early as only one year after her father's death, and then, after an unspecified amount of time, switched to Ehrlich, before coming to Agthe's former student, Kullak. This time sequence differs from *Iphigenia*, where instead of Ehrlich a Prof. Gross is mentioned (the difference in the names being too great to allow any pseudonymic connection).

18. According to Cobb, Steiniger studied with Ehrlich and then with Kullak. Cobb does not mention Prof. Gross *(Iphigenia)* and neither does *Liszts Offenbarung*, 244, according to which she studied first with Kullak for two years and then with Ehrlich for three more (confirmed in *Das Musizieren der Zukunft* Vol. 2 No. 1 [March 1912], 345, according to which Steiniger studied "for years" with Ehrlich) before meeting Deppe.

19. She describes his hands as being deformed from his own method, "the fingers turned back and over the ends like blunted sledge hammers." (*Iphigenia*, 27).

20. *Iphigenia*: before the Franco-Prussian war; Cobb: during the Franco-German war.

21. In *Iphigenia*, she met Deppe before her brother's death, while in Cobb this event triggered her search for the new method. Cobb states that Deppe came from Hamburg, while according to *Iphigenia* he directed the Dresden *Singakademie* prior to Berlin, a fact not mentioned in other bibliographical entries (or just another confusion by Clark).

22. In *Liszts Offenbarung*, 244, he tells Steiniger that no woman can think, while in *Iphigenia*, 223, we find this sentence: "Oedipus [Deppe] now thought that the young American [Clark] might indeed have the making of a man in him, if a boy, and not a girl, were first born to him."

23. Cobb, 9-10.

24. Steiniger (or Clark) mentions this deceit because when audiences in America observed her playing, they could see that she was not applying this knowledge in the manner Clark developed it: a claim which was made in Cobb in connection with the discovery of the shoulder mechanism.

25. Etelka Gerster (1855-1920) was a noted Hungarian soprano who sang in Berlin, Budapest, London (1878-80), and the United States (1880-83, 1887). According to *A Handbook of American Music and Musicians*, ed. F. O. Jones, (New York: Da Capo Press, 1971), a reprint of 1886 edition, s.v. "Steiniger-Clark, Anna," Aafke Kuypers and Anna made a successful tour of Holland, receiving distinctions from the Queen of Holland. Anna Schimon-Regan (1841-1902), German soprano, sang in Hannover, in Berlioz's concerts in St. Petersburg in 1867-68, and gave song recitals in England every winter from 1869 to 1875.

26. She recalls the first trip as bringing very bad financial results, while the second one proved better. Tired from many receptions, she often spent her time there in the company of George Eliot, Jennie Lind, and Madame Moscheles, who presented Steiniger with her husband's complete works for piano.

27. According to Cobb, 17. In *Iphigenia*, 107, Reuss was prince of Hesse (spelled "Chesse").

28. In the fall of 1883 she apparently underwent an operation in the Berlin Charity hospital, as a result of "wrong exercises" advised by Deppe, which Clark describes as "very dangerous." (*Das Musizieren der Zukunft*, Vol. 2 No. 1, March 1912, 352). Several students apparently did not endure working with Deppe, either because of mental pressure or physical ailments: Clark mentions a S. Fabian, pianist from San Francisco, and a Prof. Chas. W. Morrison, from Oberlin University. After these cases, Deppe apparently asked for a written commitment to a year-long study.

29. Carl Reinecke (1824-1910) was a renowned German pianist, composer, conductor, and pedagogue. He conducted the Gewandhaus Concerts in Leipzig for thirty-five years and taught at the Leipzig Conservatory.

30. The festival was established by Count Hochberg in 1876.

31. This is another pseudonym. Mentioned by his true name in the *Handbook of American Music and Musicians*, s.v. "Steniger-Clark, Anna," Wilhelm Gericke (1845-1925) worked in Linz and Vienna (he led Gesselschaft der Musikfreunde and Singverein) conducting the Boston Symphony Orchestra from 1884 to 1889 and from 1898 to 1906.

32. Indeed, *The Boston Symphony Orchestra*, 1881-1931 by DeWolfe Howe (Boston and New York: Houghton Mifflin, 1931), 259, lists "Steininger, Anna Clark" as having participated as a soloist in five concerts during 1885, 1886, and 1890.

33. Perhaps it was with this violinist that she played the ten sonatas of Beethoven for piano and violin which, according to the *Handbook of American Music and Musicians*, were thus performed for the first time in America (first integral performance?).

34. As confirmed in note 32, where the last year of participation mentioned is 1890.

35. The Christian Science movement was founded by Mary Baker Eddy (1821-1910). In 1866, she was healed of a serious injury as she read the account of one of Jesus' healings in the New Testament. This led her to discover what she came to understand as the Science of Christianity, which she named Christian Science. In 1875, she first wrote and published *Science and Health*

with Key to the Scriptures, the textbook of Christian Science, and in 1879 she established the Church of Christ, Scientist. In 1995, she was elected to the National Women's Hall of Fame as the only American woman to found a worldwide religion.

The Californian Kaweah Colony (The Kaweah Cooperative Commonwealth of California) centered around two charismatic persons: Charles F. Keller and Burnette Haskell, who from 1885 to 1891 tried to organize a self-sufficient utopian community. They constructed a road to the lands of the Giant Forest section in the Kaweah River watershed (forty miles east and north of Visalia), and in all their enterprises promoted an atmosphere of unfettered debate, establishing clubs, music bands, theater groups, debate societies, and experimenting with some then radical ideas, such as the referendum, initiative, and recall. Conflict with interests of larger enterprises in that area, which had sufficient political clout, brought about the colony's slow end.

In *Iphigenia,* the heroine actually expresses on several occasions a desire, later repressed in an act of self-sacrifice, to leave Mt. Desert and move westward, either to Clark's mother in Chicago or to the Kaweah Colony in California.

The interest in utopian ideas, shared by Anna Steiniger, Clark, and their small circle of friends, is confirmed by mention of a discussion they had on the novel *Looking Backward* (Boston: Ticknor, 1888) by Edward Bellamy (1850-1898). This work apparently helped to fill the void felt by Americans who desired the utopian sense of community. It addressed the yearnings of a society stricken by economic panics and social collapse by proposing an Eden-like community in which war, hunger, and malice do not exist. Its main character, Julian West, wakes up in a Boston of 2000 A.D. after 113 years of sleep.

Dickens also discussed with them the novel *Zanoni* (1842) by Edward George Earl Bulwer-Lyton (1803-73), and in particular his ideology according to which human love is antagonistic to idealism, art, and individuality. This proved to be one of the main reasons why Dr. Dickens and Anna tried to break up her own dependency on Clark and her love for him, and thus probably drove her to suicide. Bulwer-Lytton was a prolific Victorian novelist, member of Parliament, secretary of state for the colonies and a baron since 1866. His novel *Paul Clifford* (1830) set a standard for all crime-novel opening clichés: "It was a dark and stormy night . . ."

36. It is also possible that, since the last dated document in *Iphigenia* was written on 20 January 1891, and she apparently wrote the last pages of her diary on a Christmas Eve, she could have died on or right after the 1891 Christmas Eve.

37. Since Clark claims that "Iphigenia's" friends handed to him her personal papers, those friends (if not Clark himself) must have discovered her diary between 1891 and 1895.

3

Clark's Writings

A chronological survey of Clark's books and articles shows clearly the background and evolution of his philosophical and religious principles, and is necessary before a coherent presentation of his integral system of reasoning can be attempted. Only the works that provide philosophical bases and their evolution are discussed here. The works on interpretation, which demonstrate the application of the system, will be discussed in chapter 7.

Die Lehre des einheitlichen Kunstmittels beim Klavierspiel

Die Lehre des einheitlichen Kunstmittels beim Klavierspiel: eine Kritik der Claviermethoden (The doctrine of unified art of piano playing: A criticism of piano methods) of 1885 was Clark's first and, although only forty-nine pages long, probably most important work.[1] It was preceded by a "prospectus" on anatomy and physiology of piano playing that Clark apparently wrote in 1880, while in the United States. This publication (probably self-published and not registered anywhere) appeared as a reaction to Heinrich Ehrlich's[2] book *Wie übt man am Klavier* (How to practice piano), which he read in the same year. It must have already contained some physical exercises, because he mentions a particular "arm over the head" exercise, which he taught to Elisabeth Caland in February 1885. *Die Lehre* emerged then as a combination of an elaboration of those thoughts and the "revelation" he had.

In the preface, he rationalizes his need to search for a way to expose and nourish the source of the phenomenon of piano playing. This activity, when at the highest level, represents an artistic achievement and an act of creation, which often seem supernatural and inexplicable. Clark, who gave his name as "Frederic Clark-Steiniger," expressed his gratitude to, among others, Hermann Helmholtz, who apparently wrote Clark a short note expressing dissatisfaction with shortcomings of different touches on the piano. Helmholtz wrote: "As far as I see it, new [piano-]mechanisms allow only a change of speed with which the hammer attacks the string, i.e., of the force of attack on the key."[3]

Clark was motivated by the belief that nature provides mankind with means to interpret and realize the laws that allow material manifestations of our thoughts. His human and artistic credo is expressed in the following thought: "In order to subordinate execution and technique to the artistic ideas, we have to choose the form of power and movement that absolutely mirrors a continuous and progressive flow of thoughts."[4] Clark therefore regarded the body as a part of the complex unit it creates with the piano, and stressed the importance of perceiving the continuity of the muscle-action during and between playing notes. He called for a *phorolyse*[5] in playing, complaining that the other methods concentrated on the moment of tone production as the primary objective. According to him, sound was to occur as an imminent consequence of the movement, which in turn had to mediate a true picture of the logical sequence of thoughts in a musical work.

Postulating correctly that it is only by a sequence of tones that an impression of *different* touches and timbres can be conveyed, Clark asserts that it is the movement made to repeat the tone or to connect it to the next one that is the true beginning of piano technique. Contemplating this sequence, he felt the contradiction between the broken movements of a pianist's arms and the continuous motion of music. He found the model for the required continuity of movement in the motion of the earth around its axis and the sun, combined with the rotation of the sun around the weight center of the solar system, which in its turn moves forward in a straight line. When applied to the pianist, Clark saw that this rotating system described a circular sphere, the axis of which ran from a fixed point in the spine to the root (knuckle) of the middle finger, and the basis of which lay in the fingertip.[6] The mathematical formulas in chapter 2 of *Die Lehre* describe the movements of each of the members of the playing mechanism, and demand curvilinear movements, which impose themselves as the unified result of the movement of the whole mass system.

This was disputed by Breithaupt, who was provoked by Clark's demand for rotation and tension in all joints. Admitting the fact that Clark was the first to offer a graphic fixation of rolling movements, Breithaupt thought that forearm and arm rotation were confused with arm turn and that rotation axes were wrong, since in his opinion they could be considered only through wrist points. From that statement follows the conclusion that Breithaupt considered the fingers only as an appendix to the axis and the final big joint (wrist), while Clark's system apparently offered more refined control of the fingers, since their tips were also considered and used as rotation points. The axis had to change its length constantly, with help from the elbow joint, to allow moving along the keyboard. To preserve the axis, the elbow had to be on the same plane as the depressed key, and this also represented the lowest point in such a form of movement. The power of tone production and the movements for the duration of the sound were to be regulated by the elasticity of torsion along the shoulder-finger axis. The ultimate goal of these technical descriptions was to unify the contemplative action of the human mind with the organic substance (body) for a direct action upon an inorganic instrument. Clark warned that although these ideas are probably immanent to ingenious minds, like Liszt, Rubinstein, and d'Albert, they could without doubt be assimilated by anyone willing to learn and understand them. Such an accomplishment did not imply, of course, that the person using the skill would all of a sudden develop interpretative capabilities of a genius.

After ten years of research and study of the problem, guided by mathematical formulas,[7] he advocated a position of straight spine, relaxed shoulders, and a 45 degree angle of the upper arm from the torso, while maintaining the elbow-to-fingertip plane horizontal. He also considered the elasticity of shoulder muscles and shoulder blades to be of utmost importance to natural, free, and regular tone production. Describing in great detail the anatomical structure of the playing mechanism, Clark also suggested exercises to train the body, organizing them by the groups of muscles they involved.[8] Furthermore, he recognized the importance of alternating the tension and relaxation, learned by physical training, not only for strengthening of the exercised muscle, but also to avoid temporary or permanent injury (!). He concludes the book with the following statement:

> The absolute unity of the body and of the spirit, necessary for
> the expression of an idea in the reproductive art, the production
> of a conscious life in physical detail, which develops the psy-
> cho-physical consciousness, the observation of natural laws, to
> which an organ must subject itself, and, finally, the overview
> by the reason, which makes it possible to transform this into a
> momentary action of the will; all of these enable the formation
> [of unification][9] between study of art and building the charac-
> ter.[10]

With this book Clark started the slow but historically inevitable process of acquiring a consciousness of one's body, requesting full conformity with axioms such as the unity of body and soul, observation of
nature's laws, conscious physical motion, and momentary creation of
the will.

Iphigenia, Baroness of Styne

*Iphigenia, Baroness of Styne: A Story of the "Divine Impatience," an
Approximate Autobiography,*[11] allegedly based on Anna Steiniger's
recorded memories, was arranged for publication by Clark in 1896.
The book is divided into eight chapters. The first describes the pianist's childhood in great detail. Prussian family life and principles are
discussed. The social and cultural climates are depicted, and the pecu-
liar Prussian attitude toward art is presented (actually, resented). The
next chapter deals with the baroness's piano teachers. In the third
chapter, Steiniger concentrates on "Oedipus," i.e. Deppe, and describes his character, background, educational principles, and innovations in the field of piano technique. This chapter is one of the rare
sources of information about the life and work of Deppe, a person of
substantial fame in his own time, and a person who is perhaps more
known through Elisabeth Caland's "digested" versions of his school of
piano technique.[12]

When describing Deppe's ideas and working methods, "Iphigenia" was very often much more critical in qualifying his approach
than its description in John Storer Cobb's *Anna Steiniger* would suggest.[13] Whereas in Cobb full respect is given to his artistic ideas and
ideals of tone production (even by Clark), in *Iphigenia* the criticism
seems more to be Clark's own. It was certainly enhanced by the years
separating the events and the compilation of the book, and Clark's
shift toward general rejection of other methods but his own.

Deppe apparently started with the assumption that if formless flow is a basis of life, it has to be a basis of art, too.[14] Since gravitation is the most common natural law, the sound had to be produced by the phlegmatic falling of the flesh. Fingers were to be dropped passively from the knuckles (this was termed by Deppe as the "absolute technique"). There was no mention on how the finger was to be lifted, though. Those movements were, however, not organized, and Deppe regarded the "unnatural dissectivity of percussive action" as a necessary evil.[15] To develop an absolutely even and (theoretically) actionless play, Deppe started with exercises in which the hand's back was flattened, then practiced finger-dropping (soft, lifeless, passive weight of fingers), and finally legato.[16] To ensure passivity, during scale playing or extensions the wrist was to be turned outwardly from note to note. In this place, "Iphigenia" comments that this is the first mention ever of horizontal wrist movement. Clark added his footnote there, disputing this.[17] The elbow was the pivot point of arm motion and the point of greatest weight.[18]

Deppe's ideal of passivity in playing had its counterpart in his attitude towards interpretation. "Characteristic characterlessness" was for him the condition necessary in achieving the purity of music.[19] When teaching interpretation, however, Deppe was very intense, and the phlegmatic cover seems to have been very deceiving. He required absolute variety in every measure, but always resented being reminded that he was the one to demand absolute monotony in practicing the technique of the same piece. Thus it took "Iphigenia" six months to put together a Beethoven sonata following Deppe's procedures.

Deppe's ideas on art seem to have touched her the most. Art was to be a sanctuary for an artist. God was a metaphysical abstraction and so, according to Kant, man was the only personified intelligence. Therefore, while everything was to be sacrificed for art, it was to be done without religious interpretation. Deppe considered the way a key was attacked (and a tone produced) a demonstration of power and presence of pure mind or manifested spirit, because it had to be approached with absolute concentration. Good habits in playing were to be acquired by exercising discipline in everyday life. Emphasizing regularity as the basis of control, he idealized the Prussian army as an example of discipline.

"Iphigenia" (or, probably even more, Clark) found flaws in Deppe's approach from the moment she realized that his technical description and method did not work in reality and did not actually correspond to his proclaimed ideals. She still asserted that Deppe was the first to advocate (but not employ) natural laws instead of self-inveigling or open brutalism. The most serious objections were due to the lack of coordination between the form and the movement in music, and to the proclaimed (but practically implausible) passivity in tone production.[20]

According to *Iphigenia*, when Deppe was confronted with Clark's discovery of a new, anatomically-based approach, he wrote a circular as a reaction. In it he described his concept of "conscious unconsciousness" of true pianism and claimed he had always taught anatomical study and exercise. This must have been the famous article entitled *Armleiden des Klavierspielers* (Ailments of the arm among pianists), published in the *Deutsche Musiker-Zeitung* in 1885. It is the only writing by Deppe ever reaching print, and "Iphigenia" states that it is a lie, written only in reaction to Clark's disclosure of his method to Deppe. If this were true, it would put Elisabeth Caland's books on Deppe's teaching in an even more dubious light than inferred by Breithaupt and suggested by Clark himself.[21]

Working as Deppe's assistant, "Iphigenia" meets a young American, called here "Leo(pold) St. Damian." She describes him as an exotic American savage, naïve and pure, but full of inborn power. The impression seems to be realistic, especially from the perspective of the strict German and Prussian elite. Mutually attracted by sincerity and profound views on music, the couple falls in love and marries.

The sixth chapter follows the development of Damian's (or "Daemon's," as Deppe called him) ideas of motivation and muscular activity behind the mechanical act of playing the keyboard. The couple's five-year stay in the United States proves disastrous both for their new approach and for Mrs. Steiniger's health. The book ends with her death in 1890.

On Religious Education in Our Schools

A very curious publication by Clark appeared in 1897. It was entitled *On Religious Education in Our Schools, and the Christian Teaching of Music, Particularly Pianoforte Music: A Plea to Leo XIII.*[22] Consisting of 103 nine-line verses, some rhymed and some not, he offers his answer to the encyclical on education written by Pope Leo XIII on 1 August 1897 in Rome. Parts of the encyclical are given in an appendix titled "Mottoes," at the end of the pamphlet. Apart from demonstrating Clark's ever-growing interest in religion and social affairs, this work only reinforces and restates Clark's beliefs about the necessity of the harmonious development of man. Clark also criticizes the contemporary piano teachers' motives and practices. "Oh farce unmixed, to hope to reach/Those who pianoforte teach!"[23] exclaims Clark. This outcry remained as a symbol of the rest of his life, spent trying in vain to influence German educational fortresses.

Heaven or America: The Pope and Christ

In 1898 Clark published a pamphlet titled *Heaven or America: The Pope and Christ.*[24] Clark subtitled this work "Reparation of Public Scandals" and called it an open letter, an epistle, and a reply to a book entitled *America or Rome: Christ or the Pope.* The book was written by a Mr. John L. Brandt, who appears to have been the leader of the American Protective Association (APA). Brandt was spearheading Protestant endeavors to suppress the Catholic religion, and Clark, an ardent Catholic, stood up in its defense. While the contents of this pamphlet is of no particular importance to the study of his endeavors in music, its very existence is typical of some traits in Clark's character and the changes it had undergone at this time.

Clark was always a fighter for just causes, and his whole life passed in a stubborn attempt to bring out the truth as he saw it. His acute sense of social awareness developed even more with the poor living conditions that he and his family apparently endured. Social injustice, corruption, and elitism always disturbed him very much, but especially after his last American experiences and the death of his first wife. Urging the reader to stand up for American patriotism and freedom in choice of religion, Clark saw the work of the APA as resulting from purposeful misunderstanding and misinterpretation of Christ's life and teaching. He urged all men to enjoy the absolute and visible unity of genuine Christian freedom. Clark upheld harmony everywhere and expressed shock over violence in any form, especially as a result of religious provincialism. This tendency towards absolute harmony with the surrounding world and with the world within apparently stemmed from his ever-deeper immersion into religion, philosophy, and metaphysics.

Ein alter Brief an Liszt

This twelve-page "Old Letter to Liszt" was supposedly written in February 1883, in Berlin and London, as indicated at its end.[25] This is also the only source that tells us Clark was in London for the second time, almost a year after his marriage. In the introduction Clark mentions that after the first occasion he heard Liszt play he always wanted to interpret his playing in scientific terms, an enterprise that at the time of the writing of this letter was already going on for seven years (they supposedly met for the first time in 1877). The central theme of the letter is the sentence supposedly coming from Liszt, which Clark frequently quoted in his other works:

> The technique is formed from the mechanics of the spirit, not from the mechanics of piano. One should take the mechanics of the universe as an example of the true freedom in the mechanics of piano-playing![26]

The rest of this letter reads like a compendium of Clark's basic thoughts, and therefore provides a succinct recapitulation of his reasoning.

Thus, according to Clark, pure legato playing should be conceived as a harmonious activity resulting from an impulse system, starting with the heart, spinal column, and shoulder blade, continuing through the extremities. He claims that it is absolutely impossible to utilize a single member that belongs to a system (such as upper arm or forearm) in a free, fluent manner without it being moved in a spherical, oscillating, longitudinal (i.e., progressing on all planes) movement. The only possibility for a true legato lies thus in coordinating those oscillations in regular proportions. Clark insists that this coordination provides the strength of the spiritual freedom of music making. In his own words: "The system of constant activity, the source of legato, depends for its maintenance on the amalgamation of the cycloids formed by the spiral movements of all kinds and varieties of the participating members."[27] Clark continuously emphasizes that any isolated member activity negates the true *Harmonie*, which by its definition means bringing together, but not without interdependence. Harmony is, therefore, a "binding of variety."

In the letter we find also an interesting argument for the use of the word "musiciring," which he employs very frequently in his writings, and which on first sight appears simply to be a bad translation from

German (*musizieren*). Apparently he insists on this word to avoid the term "playing" which has the connotations of a childish and unconscious act.

Clark also tries to make the case for piano as the only instrument that offers the opportunity to employ this "principle of the harmonization of the will." Only true legato playing on the piano, according to Clark, gives the opportunity to develop the creative aspect that should be "the goal of any scientific and esthetical pedagogy of piano-playing."[28] Clark asserts that Liszt has already accomplished this in an unsurpassable manner that, unfortunately, remains hidden and inexplicable to the eyes of others.

Liszts Offenbarung

Liszts Offenbarung: Schlüssel zur Freiheit des Individuums (Liszts revelation: Key to the freedom of the individual) was published in Berlin in 1907.[29] The book deals mostly with Clark's own experiences in Europe. Describing his youth in America and pilgrimage to Liszt in Europe, Clark seems to be convinced that his urge to meet Liszt was a "divine command." The second chapter describes at length Liszt's philosophy. Clark states that Liszt summarized all the ideas of the individuality in human spirit occurring in different philosophical schools, and found their culmination in the teachings of Christianity. Furthermore, Liszt considered the modern evolution theory as the foundation of the "scientific religion" in the development of the arts.[30] In the next chapter, Liszt's achievements in piano technique are explained, supposedly in his own words. They were based on an introduction of absolute harmony as the manifestation of free-will unity with the "absolute law" (*logos*), denoting the universal principle of life.

According to the book, upon hearing Liszt play, Clark became more and more aware of the notion of freedom of organic will, which can be realized only in the course of harmonic activity. In chapter 5, Clark makes it clear that Liszt was very much aware of the uniqueness and quality of his achievements. Clark explains that Liszt saw himself as a creator, forming live shapes with his playing and essentially recreating the spiritual essence of Christianity. Although during Liszt's lifetime academic institutions were generally fortresses of conservatism, most of the "Herr Professors" carefully observed Liszt's achievements. Openly or not, they had to admit that the profoundness, sincerity, and wholesomeness of the approach were unprecedented, and could not be practically disputed.

Clark continues with a description of his experience as a student in Liszt's class. He observed with the eyes of a physiologist, and made conclusions of a practical philosopher. More than fifty pages are devoted to what he calls false prophecies, fashionable theories, superficial methods, and all types of deluding ideas. According to Clark, these obscure the only feasible, universal, harmonic, and cosmological law, following which true art can be perpetrated.

The comparison between Liszt's and Deppe's ideas is especially interesting. Liszt was the first to reject the "strike-and-fall" approach, so common at the time and emulating the mechanical action of the instrument. Deppe, however, was the one to proclaim the new ideal and deny any activity at the keyboard—a procedure Clark calls "falling apart in oneself."[31] While Liszt was trying to use legato in a way in which the mechanics of the instrument would not influence the player's technique, Deppe sought to escape the piano's mechanical restrictions by imitating the action of the instrument. His ideal was to round out individual tones, and then organize them by perfectly even and unchanged reproduction of the movement for the following tones.[32] According to Clark, Deppe was trying to emulate the spirit of Spohr, a so-called "sweet naiveté." Deppe required complete perfection in the execution of his exercises and scale playing before he ever started to explain interpretation. Therefore, Clark concludes, Deppe did not realize the necessity of understanding form and making it the reason for a specific practice and employment of tone building and technique.[33] Deppe's "free fall" technique makes the sound—in other words the material—the starting point, while Liszt sought to incorporate the technique in the spirit, making technique a truly spiritual force.

At the end of *Liszts Offenbarung* (chapter 9), Clark, now mature, departs from Liszt. During their final conversation, Liszt reiterated the importance of his "religious art," and made obvious that the inclination toward and acceptance of universal harmony were the foundation for a self-conscious integrating of man's will with universal (cosmic, religious) will.

Pianistenharmonie

Understandably enough, upon being criticized, ignored, and almost ostracized after attempting to share his discoveries and make them public, Clark's theory grew more and more enclosed, self-satisfactory, and hermetic. Only three years after the book on Liszt, Clark completed *Pianistenharmonie* (1910), in which he perfects and concludes the theory supporting his piano method. On the one hand, he really improved the theory underlying his method. On the other, the religion of mankind became religion in its narrower sense and retreated into the sphere of philosophical causality, as explained in Leibniz's Monad no. 81.[34] Attempting to achieve absolute harmony of the body and soul, Clark idealized the notion of self-purposed motion (since all that is perfect is self-purposed). He warned that "self-purposeness" could lead either to individuality or universality, depending upon the approach.

In a parallel German-English edition, he assesses the universal task of a true artist: to evolve a free unifying process of work and thought, aspiring toward perfection. He is influenced in this idea by St. Thomas, according to whom it is a Christian virtue to strive perpetually to understand and realize the right action. Such an intricate order of individualizing freedom, when realized fully imitates the Creator's actions—a vortex of self-activity, as Clark explains it. A blending of contrasts creates a concordance that, elevated to a universal level, signifies life and harmony. Trying to establish a relationship between ethics, religion, and beauty, Clark regards beauty as a universal category, blending people with God and the universe. The nobility of music is achieved only through its ethical and religious connotations.

If, as Plato states, man's powers are not unified in organic will, objectiveness remains incomplete, and harmony and freedom of beauty can not evolve.[35] According to Clark, will should always be creative and self-determining. In the book he introduces Aristotle's term *entelechy*, the organizing energy of the soul, working to manifest and perfect an individuality of the forms of life. Being a pure activity, the energy is necessarily perpetual. For Clark, *Harmonie* is the source and the end of a being; therefore it is life itself, and the soul its reflection. Aristotle teaches that an imperfect motion aims at an external, foreign point and also ends there.[36] Perfect motion, on the contrary, has its aim in itself and so is perpetuated endlessly.

For the practical model of this concept Clark chose the solar system model, where each globe (point) rotates in itself in harmony with others, displaying a universal unification of force and motion. Since the perfect motion of each globe is self-purposed and all globes are self-purposed, then the system's harmony is also self-purposed.

Clark saw this model as a mirror of God's individuality unto and within us. Accordingly, he maintains that performances with imperfect motions achieve only an outer form. Imperfect motion cannot result in a true artistic performance.

In the last chapter (chapter 7), Clark presents historical cases of *Harmonie* realized to a different extent in the lives of Moses, Plato, David, Aristotle, Christ, James, and John. In addition to the text, Clark includes pictures of his own patented "*Harmonie*-piano," constructed to realize his theory.[37]

Brahms' Noblesse

Clark's last published work seems to be *Brahms' Noblesse*.[38] On more than four hundred pages, again in both German and English, organized into thirty-three chapters plus appendices, he elaborates his "*Harmonie*-method," connecting it this time with Johannes Brahms. The degree to which Clark makes Brahms's doctrine dependent on Catholic religion and to which it fits Clark's system, and the fact that he reports, apparently word for word and on almost two hundred pages, events that took place thirty-five years ago, make this book even less plausible as a whole than *Liszts Offenbarung*. The work seems to be more of a desperate final attempt to reach out with his message, trying to break through the tacit rejection of his colleagues by lending to his words an additional weight of a musical authority. Even so, it represents a valid source of study in order to complete the philosophical—now basically metaphysical—tenets of his system.

He starts with events from his childhood that have made him attentive to the notion of harmony, solar system motion, and re-creation of god-like self-purposed activity. Remaining in partial congruity with his biography, Clark describes his meeting with Brahms in an old hotel in Hamburg, where he had just arrived from the United States. Brahms was presented to him as "composer and faithful friend of the landlord and former pianist of the hotel"[39]—a not utterly unbelievable claim. Brahms showed Clark the double piano that he was trying out.[40] It consisted essentially of two separate and parallel mirroring shoulder-high keyboards. The theory behind the design of the piano underlies what Brahms called the "Cherubim-doctrine," with the notion of the cherubim as God's musicians. The wielding of arms on both sides of a cherub that he was practicing (Clark's interpretation) was centralized in the solar plexus and heart, so that in his actions he realized the balance and central control of the higher harmony.[41] He considered through his approach the blending with the universal as the primary motive, and "musiciring" only a secondary by-product.[42] Brahms relates that he got the idea of the shoulder-high, inclined keyboard while struggling to reach the second and third row of keys on a church organ.

A long chapter is dedicated to an attack on Deppe's method. According to Clark, Brahms thought that Deppe took from Rubinstein the very idea of weight playing as a mere reaction to the contemporary habit of hammering the keys, but Deppe still considered the pianist only from elbow to knuckles. Deppe's method was also a descendant of the Bach method, with a low seat, in order to get the movements of elbow and hand isolated from finger action. Brahms was aware of the fact that Bach's method and sitting habits were targets of caricatures and jokes, even in Bach's own lifetime. Trying to conform the playing mechanism to the ever-present force of gravity, Deppe still did not offer a conscious way of dealing with it, but rather remained consciously unconscious about it.

Brahms continues by enumerating precisely, but rather redundantly, the so-called "forty-seven extremes" of a pianist. Extremes representing all angles and extreme positions that lead to broken movements are thus divided: ten of position, including knees, hips, and all angles in the usual posture at the piano; ten of separation in work, including lack of coordination, disorder, independence of members; twelve of movement, pertaining to chaos in the organization of horizontal and vertical plains of axis in play; and finally fifteen of power, summarizing all forceful, hammering, strenuous, and strength-deploying kinds of attack on the keyboard. Brahms concludes his narration with a precise definition of the *Pianistenharmonie*: "*Pianistenharmonie* is the germ of true religion, art, and education blended in one mode of soul's expression and perfection of body and mind, . . . peace and freedom of the individual."[43]

The appendices of the book contain Clark's second letter to Kaiser Wilhelm II (already mentioned above), two advertisements for concerts on the new piano, some reviews of Clark's concerts, and the editions published or planned in the *Pianistenharmoniepresse*. The letter helps clarify some details in Clark's biography, such as the fact that he had apparently already had a vision of the double-keyboard piano in 1885, but was advised by his friends not to reveal it for a while. This in a way corresponds to the alleged story with Brahms, where Brahms asked him, after their conversation, never to speak of the experiments and the related philosophy during Brahms's lifetime.

Notes

1. (Berlin: Raabe & Plothow, 1885).

2. Heinrich Ehrlich (1822-1899), Austrian pianist and writer, was a pupil of Henselt and Thalberg. He taught at the Stern Conservatory in Berlin and was also music critic of the *Berliner Tageblatt*.

3. *Die Lehre*, 4. In the original: "Soweit ich sehe, kann bei den neueren Mechanismen nur der Geschwindigkeitsgrad, mit welchem der Hammer gegen die Saite fliegt, d. h. die Kraft des Anschlags von der Taste aus modificirt werden."

4. *Die Lehre*, 8. (Wollen wir Vortrag mit Technik vereint dem künstlerischen Gedanken unterordnen, so können wir dieses nur durch Wahl einer Form der Kraft und Bewegung, welche dem zeitlich continuirlich fortschreitenden Lauf des Gedankens absolut entspricht.)

5. This term was an object of ridicule in a review of this method written by Heinrich Dorn. The review, consisting of several pages, appeared, according to Clark's *Iphigenia, Baroness of Styne: A Story of the "Divine Impatience," an Approximate Autobiography* (n.p.: Pure Music Society, priv. ed., 1896), 245-46, in *Bote und Bock's Magazin*, and might have also been a reaction to the article Clark had written for the *Charlottenburg-Inteligenzblatt*. The term itself was described in *Liszts Offenbarung*, 301, as the analysis of motion and criticism of methods.

6. Here Clark calls again on Helmholtz, who, as Clark states, had recently proved that fingers can participate in torsion (*Die Lehre*, 12). Also, it seems that motivated by Clark's initiative in 1905, a Prof. Dr. Fischer published in 1907 a work called *Kinematik organischer Gelenke*, in which there is a mathematically-based introduction on the spherical movement capacity of members.

7. The formulas were elaborated by a Mr. H. Wilhelm. The chapter with mathematical formulas was described by Dorn in the above-mentioned review as mistakenly taken from a book on tea-making (!):

> St. Damian (the pseudonym Clark used for himself in *Iphigenia*) is a great comedian, and is playing a prime joke on the world; best of all, the printer in binding his brochure has, by mistake, included as a large portion thereof, a chapter on tea-making which was the belonging of an advertisement for a

Japanese bazaar on the Leipziger street, Berlin! (*Iphigenia*, 245)

In *Das Musizieren der Zukunft*, Vol. 1 No. 4 (December 1907), 231, he refers to this review again, this time mentioning a "Chinese" tea-merchant. In the preface of the book, Clark also express gratitude to Prof. Robert Hartmann for the anatomical arm preparations he used. The anatomical drawings were borrowed from Hermann Meyer's *Lehrbuch der Anatomie*.

8. Clark must have realized the importance of proper physical preparation already as a student: according to his journal *Das Musizieren der Zukunft* Vol. 2 No. 1 (March 1912), 352, his first teacher's (Dr. Oscar Paul) physician, a Dr. Kurzwelly, advised him to return to America because of the weakness of his upper torso and arms. Oskar Paul himself gave him physical exercises for development of the upper body during three years, and when he returned to Germany in 1880 to study with Prof. Ehrlich in Berlin, Ehrlich helped him install some exercise utensils in the room where he was staying. According to Clark, Deppe's claim regarding his recommendation of physical exercises came only as a reaction to the appearance of Clark's book. See chapter 9.

9. Added here in handwriting, probably Clark's own, in a copy presented to the library of Princeton University by the author.

10. *Die Lehre*, 49. Probably referring to the process of formation and maturation of an individual.

11. (n.p.: Pure Music Society, priv. ed., 1896).

12. As described above in chapter 1, note 69, Clark asserts that Caland stole his ideas and introduced them as her own, interspersing them with those coming from Ludwig Deppe, the person she was actually writing about. See chapter 9.

13. John Storer Cobb, *Anna Steiniger, a Biographical Sketch: In Which Is Contained a Suggestion of the Clark-Steiniger System of Piano-forte Playing* (Boston: Schirmer, 1886).

14. This is a rather dangerous thought, for it implies that the natural state of matter is without any intrinsic order. Although philosophically and cosmologically plausible, this state would then lead progressively, following imminent entropy, to chaos. How he could have hoped to reproduce art without a means of organization, or whether he realized the inherent paradox, is an issue that needs further clarification.

15. *Iphigenia*, 56.

16. "The hands were to be held over the keyboard in devitalized position until they fell trembling down into the lap." *Iphigenia*, 208.

17. This is how Clark corrected "Iphigenia" (or simply tried to make the book more plausible and her identity more realistic, by appearing to contradict her opinion):

Our autobiographist has evidently written this under impressions received from her hero of the hour, the experience of which she is portraying in ignorance of the fact that the horizontal motion was thoroughly inculcated by Louis Kohler long before "Oedipus's" [Deppe's] Berlin period, and was, with adequate science as to the expression of his intentions published by him as early as 1840 in his celebrated *Theory of Pianism* dedicated to Franz Liszt." (*Iphigenia*, 65)

18. That had to cause quite a tension in the wrist region to compensate if the fingers were to remain passive.

19. *Iphigenia*, 53. This could be also interpreted as a very early attempt to express a sacrifice of individual interpretation for the sake of music's objectivity.

20. "Iphigenia" criticizes: "Indeed! Is not this as if the nature of life was manifested not in life but in death and as if natural law lay not in universal attractivity but in special cohesion!" (*Iphigenia*, 55)

21. This issue was already addressed in chapter 1 (note 69) and will be further analyzed in chapter 9.

22. This poetic pamphlet was published in October 1897, apparently by Clark himself. Both Chicago, Illinois, and Valparaiso, Indiana, are given as his places of residence.

23. *Religious Education*, lviii.

24. (n.p.: Society of the Sacred Heart, 1898). The work is dated at the end as being written (or published?) in Valparaiso, Indiana, on 20 November 1898. The date on the inside cover is October 1898, however. This corresponds to W. S. B. Mathews's claim that Clark was sharing his time between Valparaiso (teaching) and Chicago.

25. Frederic Horace Clark, *Ein alter Brief an Liszt*, Musikalisches Wochenblatt 35 (Leipzig, August 30, 1906; repr., Leipzig: Röder, n.d.). Its subtitle is *Über das wahre Legatospiel* (On the True Legato-Playing).

26. In the original: "Aus der Mechanik des Geistes schaffe sich die Technik, nicht aus der Mechanik des Klaviers! Man nehme die Mechanik des Weltalls zum Vorbild der wahren Freiheit in der Mechanik des Klavierspiels!" (*Ein alter Brief an Liszt*, 3)

27. *Ein alter Brief an Liszt*, 9.

28. *Ein alter Brief an Liszt*, 12.

29. Berlin: C. F. Vieweg, 1907.

30. Not to be confused with the "religion of science" of the twentieth century.

31. *Liszts Offenbarung*, 239. "In-sich-selber-Auseinanderfallen."

32. This idea appears nebulous and subjective and has no support in modern theory.

33. This is a very progressive idea.

34. Leibniz, *Monadology*, trans. George Martin Duncan (New Haven: Tuttle, Morehouse & Taylor, 1890), 230. Pre-established harmony is ex-

plained there as an interaction of two bodies (in Clark: human body and soul) that act separately, but which determine each other's actions.

35. Plato, *Republic*, 6:504.

36. Aristotle, *Metaphores*, 1050.

37. This piano is based on one inclined keyboard, as opposed to his later models. One of the explanations of the inclination is also to avoid extremes in positions.

38. Frederic Horace Clark, *Brahms' Noblesse* (Zürich: Pianisten-harmoniepresse, 1914).

39. *Brahms' Noblesse*, 29.

40. The caption of the accompanying photograph states: "Brahms trying out the 'golden-mean' keyboard," while the person in the photo is obviously Clark. He used an almost identical photo of the same instrument (actually, just two keyboards on stands, without mechanisms), taken obviously on the same occasion, in *Das Musizieren der Zukunft* (Vol. 2 No. 1, September 1912: 362), this time not implying it was Brahms on the photo.

41. A comparison to da Vinci's "golden triangle" is almost inevitable. It should be noted that Clark constantly refers to "cherubim" as a "he," although this is a plural form of "cherub."

42. Clark's English in general seems to be either very archaic or literally translated from German. Although he himself has, as mentioned above, on p. 45, sought to justify the use of the words "musiciring," other words, like "vorticing," as well as numerous misspellings, can be found throughout his books.

43. *Brahms' Noblesse*, 349.

4

The Religion and the Science of the "Cherubim-Doctrine" and of the Harmonie

The philosophical and speculative ideas which, over the years, brought Clark to the development of a unique artistic doctrine were embedded in his mind from early childhood. He often heard from his parents the words of David ("The Lord is my light"), Christ ("God is Light"), and Socrates ("The sun I name the child of God, of Good. And as in the realm of spiritual light all is focalized as the sun, . . . even so in the realm of sense, does the sun form the eye for focalizing, and in the realm of soul, the perfect will and the body unto unifying work").[1] Clark therefore often equated God with light and revered light as the image of God in one's body.

Another one of the earliest ideas with which Clark was imbued was the explanation of the first biblical sin as scorning the image of God in a human body. In an attempt to restore this reverence, Clark saw the cherubim, God's and Eden's guardians, as a perfect metaphor for action that truly pleases, imitates, and emanates from the image of godlike action itself. Also, probably at the age of twelve, he was given a picture by his father, representing the cherubim wielding the swords of fire.[2]

Since the cherubim were the guardians of Eden and God's intentions, Clark wanted to perform music in a similar godlike manner that would mirror these actions in a material world while recreating and preserving the idea of unification with godliness in a human being. Although, according to Clark, Jesus and Moses were already teaching that this "realistic"[3] love of God should be the main human objective, Clark observed that this objective had as yet not been attained. Pointing out that the yearning to blend one's body and soul with the perfect motion of God's will is eternal, Clark maintained that the age in which he lived already provided the modern technique which could, for the first time, enable the realization of the idea.

The two main elements combined in the following manner: the continuity of the light as a source and spiritual concept was to be the model for the continuing working motion of the body, while from the picture of a cherub, with its outstretched arms, and possibly because of the spiritual allegory, Clark envisioned the center of that activity in the solar plexus area.[4] Therefore, it is obvious that the "Cherubim-doctrine," as explained in Clark's final stage of development, draws heavily from the plethora of formative, philosophical, and theosophical influences to which Clark was exposed during the first fifty years of his life. It strives to recreate the old Greek principle of the golden mean by blending through this posture all extensors and flexors into one unbroken vortex-like motion.

As the next step, Clark tried to envision how this could be applied to piano playing.[5] A pianist's actions had to preserve the principles of unity and organic work. Guided by the image of concentric motion of the cherubim's arms and the solar plexus as the geometric source of this motion, Clark drew the analogy with the solar system as a model of perfect organization that followed God's intention, being indeed created by God. It was thus imperative that a player's arms describe concentric, irradiating movements which, according to Clark, would result in a pure application of motion. This was to be the realization of the freedom—muscular as well as spiritual—of an individual, achieved by mirroring the continuous, unifying, and all-encompassing action of God. Apparently, while still a child, Clark experimented with sitting on the floor in front of the piano and feeling the freedom in the direct transfer of impulses from the spine to the fingertips.[6]

Another, quite material, source for his speculations were the technical innovations of the time. His father explained to him the action of ship screws (propellers), based on studies of eagles' shoulderblades, and the propellant power resulting from a perpetual impulse. It is possible that, even for a child, the striking effect of a purely visual aesthetic pleasure of looking at such a perpetuum-mobile type of motion would result in an image sufficiently vivid to instigate a chain of ideas—even more so knowing Clark's aesthetic sensibility.

Regarding any practical application (in a correct harmonic context) only as a reflection of a larger-scale order, Clark maintains that the proper understanding of the character and identity of any live being and any inanimate object leads to the understanding of the universal world order. This order reflects in turn the work and the will of God. Therefore, while playing, one attains Harmonies (and *Harmonie*)[7] by employing kinetic systems of the body. Demonstrating the movements of the systems by observing an asp tree in the wind, his granduncle invoked the image that would follow Clark throughout his life: movement cycles multiplying in inverse proportion to the size of levers (members) involved.[8] Clark realized early on that proportional activity, conducted in harmonic ratios, was the clue to successful coordination.[9] Therefore, although free, the motions were to be always organized in an enveloping shape. This also kept the motions curved and spiraling, and never straight or angular. To reinforce this idea, Clark mentions Hezekial's vision of a cherub, as described in the Bible.[10]

Starting the movement with big groups of muscles, which are easiest to innervate, Clark voluntarily transferred their rotating momentum to smaller and smaller units, which are more difficult to control but easier to move quickly. The resulting scheme, in proportions, is the following: 1 elliptic torso motion : 2 rotary arm motions : 4 double-curve forearm motions : 8/16 epi-cycloidal hand motions. Clark relates this four-folded rotation of shoulders, elbows, and wrists to the elements of musical form—strophe, phrase, and motive—an important relationship (to be discussed in chapter 7).

In *Iphigenia*[11] Clark describes the vision that had generated his 1885 book *Die Lehre des einheitlichen Kunstmittels beim Klavier-spiel*:

> And just so as our power of grouping by one effort of blending, combines words by the swing or rhythm of phrase and sentence, so must the arm and body by their motions, make the larger rhythms and the massings of rhythms, the phrase rhythm and the sentence or line or verse-rhythm of the music as we flowingly work on the pianoforte. By envelopement! By envelopement of motions! Yes! Now I see it. . . . Envelopements, enfoldments can indeed unfold, and music is created in form-unfoldings of tone even as the universe is manifested in spherically harmonizing evolvings of force; for mortal life is ever the

expression by inversion, of idea which otherwise remains un-
born to palpable being.[12]

Clark's idea of three times enfolded (as in the Trinity) unity of three-
enfoldings[13] also became a flexible means of organizing motions
according to the inner structure of an eight-measure musical phrase.
Generally, the upper arm was to make one round for four measures,
with the pronation of the forearm dominant in the first and the third
measures and the supination in the second and in the fourth. Hands
were to describe cycles according to each motive or measure.[14] The
molten triple-spiraling proportional motion was to evolve from the
organic "fertility stemming from inner necessity,"[15] as it is almost
impossible to achieve the involvement and concentration necessary to
obtain a level of self-control that would enable the performance of
such a seemingly complex maze of movements.

Related to the "Cherubim-doctrine" is the principle of *Harmonie*.
In its broadest definition, it concerns the relationship between a human
individual, with his inner and outer life and manifestations, and God, a
divine entity whose principles of creation and perpetration have to be
mirrored in a human individual's action, if *Harmonie* is to be achieved.
Clark probably assimilated this hierarchical order from intensive study
of Hellenistic philosophy. He held firm to Aristotle's definition of
freedom and beauty as elevated harmonic developments.[16]

Also, Plotinus, sharing Plato's views, writes as the most important
representative of the Neo-Platonic movement: "The material thing
becomes beautiful—by communicating in the thought that flows from
the Divine. . . . Thus all music . . . must be earthly representation of the
music there is in the rhythm of the ideal Realm."[17] Greek "harmonics"
was the science of proportioned sounds and a symbol of universal
order. It also represented the idea of "microcosm" and "macrocosm"
as two units containing the same elements and being ruled by the same
principles. Their implicit harmony[18] holds the universe together. A free
translation of Clark's German quotation of Aristotle's' "harmony-
problem n° 38" states that we are encouraged to work by the
symphony of movements because it is a mixture or "compro-
mise/composition"[19] of the opposites, which influence each other in a
certain proportion; and symmetry of many opposites is preferable to
simple symmetry.[20] Clark states that the rotating system of cycloids
was already described by Aristotle (in *Metaphysics*), by Helmholtz
(his 1858 *Wirbeltheorie*[21]) and Geißler (*Philosophie des Unendlichen
— [Philosophy of the endless]).[22]

Bishop Isidor of Seville wrote in the seventh century: "But every word we speak, every pulsation of our veins, is related by musical rhythms to the powers of harmony. . . . The man . . . deprived of harmony does not exist."[23] In John Dryden's "A Song for St. Cecilia's Day, 1687" we find these verses: "From harmony, from heavenly harmony,/This universal frame began:/From harmony to harmony/ Through all the compass of the notes it ran,/The diapason closing full in Man."[24] Clark also quotes Goethe, according to who ". . . [if] you find in one the many, feel the many as one; and you have the beginning, and the end of art.[25]

Reading Clark's words:

> It was clear to me in this moment, that I should find such a mode of musiciring [*sic*], whereby my arms would fully, freely, wholly, develop themselves, *as if they reproduced the very light of the sun* [italics added], and that my will would thus accomplish its highest, noblest destiny on earth and my body thus learn to know and exercise the image of God within it![26]

one can immediately relate to the ideas of a whole stream of philosophers, starting in the fifth century with Christian Platonists, thirteenth-century authors Robert Grosseteste, St. Bonaventure, St. Thomas Aquinas, and others. They basically equated light, radiance, clarity, or color, with beauty. Light, harmony, and radiance were often mentioned as essential characteristics of beauty and concord *(consonantia)*. Ulrich of Strassburg, Aquinas's fellow student, added: ". . . intellectual light is the formal cause of all substantial form and all material form."[27]

A slightly different source for this doctrine is found in the words of Clark's granduncle. According to him, each body contains harmony. The variations in its purity and clarity make it correspond with related *Harmonies* in flowers, people, or music. The emphasis of this correspondence is love and, according to the Bible, God is love. Music, perceived as God's word, which is invoked by human activity, offers an absolute organization of harmony. It is therefore the most ingratiating and fit activity in which a mirroring of one's soul can be obtained. It offers the possibility for exercising love as an act of spiritual godliness, and results in a more fulfilling unity with God. Instrumental music in general, and piano playing in particular, come closest to a true harmonic activity, but only when the actions of the mind, emotions, and body are fully coordinated. In *Liszts Offenbarung*, Clark ascribes to Liszt the definition of *Harmonie* as "proportional oscillation of [in] kinematical [*sic*] freedom,"[28] and the only way the soul can mirror the principle of divine work of applied *Harmonie*, becoming thus the key to the freedom of an individual. If Clark is to be believed, he had a conversation with Royal Chancellor Bismarck in the garden of his Palace in Wilhelmstraße, during which Bismarck told him that "unity must become the politics, religion, culture and life of the German people. Who gives us unity in work, the freedom of technique, gives us everything."[29]

A doctrine based on a very individual and particular interpretation of fundamental Christian beliefs can represent, at best, an exclusive and restrictive point of view. If such a doctrine were designated as a theoretical foundation for a practical method of playing an instrument, its validity and the plausibility of its practical transfer to instrumental performance would appear to be highly questionable. Clark did not seem to be disturbed by the fact that his initial postulates come from the very extremes of the speculative mind combined with scientific research. He apparently believed that the act of simulation of godlike activity enabled and justified the reconciliation of those extremes. The simulation itself represented an act of love toward and harmony with the Creator.

This was the ideal for him, and he himself needed several years before he could play easy pieces in complete conscious control of the mind and body. But by achieving this complete involvement and merging with the idiomatic and structural tissue of a work, he claimed to have acquired absolute freedom of the individual will, and unity of body and soul. Clark's faith in his method did not come from the conviction that he was the one to show something to the world, but rather that he was happy and lucky to be chosen as a tool of Providence. He himself worked very hard, experimenting and playing, and although the results seemed to be worth the effort, he had many difficulties fighting the inert, conservative minds of what he saw as the "consecrated" caste of piano professors.

In trying to shape his own life to follow the *Harmonie* between the microcosm and the macrocosm, Clark evidently admitted all the evidence that could find a harmonic place in the overall mosaic of this relationship. Science and religion found equally important places in his philosophy. This "acquiescing" approach is also evident from his other works, such as the essay *The Philosophy of Pianoforte Music.*[30] In it, Clark sought to establish a balanced relationship between science on one side, and philosophy and intuition on the other. The techno-logical analysis of the pianists' apparatus and its efficiency in translating the principle of harmony, unity, and universality had to be combined with the morphological analysis of the principles themselves. Both of these were to add up to a complete study of the philosophy of art in general or any of the artistic disciplines in particular. Without any presumptuousness, Clark was willing to guide the human race in learning how to live by *Harmonie*. He expressed a strong belief in the power of the human brain, human inventiveness, and scientific research. Obviously he attempted to blend scientific principles with religious postulates, in what one might call an original humanistic approach. Revived and reapplied old classical Hellenistic ideals and philosophy are interpreted through a hierarchical constellation in which human actions mirror divine actions. This seems to be an apparently paradoxical relationship, directly opposing Renaissance human self-centeredness. At the same time, Clark adds to it an advanced idea of macrocosmic unification, or universality of human purpose. He writes, "If the churches would thus scientifically worship Jesus as God of progressive evolution of the individual soul (mind and body) ideal of scientific new-births in Cherubic work . . ."[31] Apparently he was prompted to attempt this fusion by the words of Franz Liszt, who, according to Clark, considered the modern evolution theory (probably meaning Charles Darwin's) as the foundation of the "scientific religion" in the development of the arts.

It is almost impossible to make out if Clark's first ideas and discoveries were already a result of such a religious involvement. In his later writings he claims they were. But it is also possible that those writings,[32] dealing with his youth, were suffused with his ideas from the period when he wrote them, rather than with his original thoughts. Be it as may be, the first book Clark wrote is the only one that does not bear an immediate relation to a religious concept. *Die Lehre des einheitlichen Kunstmittels beim Klavierspiel* was quite likely Clark's most important contribution to the development of piano technique.

During Clark's last years, religion and its hierarchic design became the final model for his theory. Moreover, there was a distinctive shift in orientation from cosmological and astronomical models to the philosophy of religion and fulfillment of man's role on earth. The latter was to be achieved in concordance with Christian parameters, because Clark was convinced that an individual soul fulfills its original purpose and acquires its spiritual nobility only by re-creating in itself the ultimate scheme of Christian organization and doctrine.

Notes

1. From Plato, *Republic*, 6, as quoted by Clark in *Brahms' Noblesse* (Zürich: Pianistenharmonie-presse, 1914), 5.

2. Writing his memories forty years later, he describes it using a very unchildlike vocabulary: "This picture represented the Cherubim as his arms performed sunlike, solar-system work with the flaming swords of fire, thus realising the heavenly will, which alone may educate Godlikeness in man's entire being." (*Brahms' Noblesse*, 5, 7)

3. This probably means: imitating and blending with the godlike principle.

4. See Da Vinci's "Golden Triangle"; also "Macrocosm and Microcosm," the title page from Robert Fludd's *Utriusque cosmi . . . historia* (Oppenheim, 1617-19), in Lewis Rowell, *Thinking About Music* (Amherst: University of Massachusetts Press, 1983; 2nd paperback ed., 1987), 42.

5. Clark denied to other instruments the capacity for harmonious action, because, according to him, they could be played only using back-and-forth movements, rather than cycloids.

6. Frederic Horace Clark, *Liszts Offenbarung: Schlüssel zur Freiheit des Individuums* (Berlin: C. F. Vieweg, 1907), 218.

7. Throughout *Brahms' Noblesse* he describes *Harmonie* or *Pianisten-harmonie* as being devoid of separate hammering activity and extremities bent at sharp angles, and thus representing the only way the soul can express the principle of divine work of the applied *Harmonie*.

8. Frederic Horace Clark, *Liszts Offenbarung: Schlüssel zur Freiheit des Individuums* (Berlin: C. F. Vieweg, 1907), 8.

9. Frederic Horace Clark, *Iphigenia, Baroness of Styne: A Story of the "Divine Impatience," an Approximate Autobiography* (n.p.: Pure Music Society, priv. ed., 1896), 232-33:

> The hand must roll like a ball, the fingers are mere rods which the ball rolls to and from the keys in its spiraly-motivating [*sic*] motion. The arm also cycling, and the torso in similar free routes, these all shall gain full working on the keys through compound polaric influence, when tensioned joints articulate merely enough to conserve the one effort musical, for the welding and differentiating of its extensions unific [*sic*]. But envelopment and harmony imply ratio and number; one cycle of arm, two of forearm, four of hand, in one and the same large unit or measure of time . . . . The work which artist's mind and will would do, if that mind be of harmonic idea, may never be harmonic work until the mass or body which the will propels be coordinately, correspondently [*sic*], confluentially harmonic.

10. *Brahms' Noblesse*, 65:

As the spirit of God came in utmost perfection upon this being (Cherubim) . . . (a being so manifold, that it appeared like a lion and eagle as well as a man). Hesekial [*sic*] saw this motion of the wings (arms) and hands (wheels) as fourfold vorticing, proportionate blending of cycloids or spiralisings, as the wheels of time and of life, coursing their endless lines, progressing ever onwards. (Hes. I. X)

11. *Iphigenia*, 226.

12. Frederic Horace Clark, *Die Lehre des einheitlichen Kunstmittels beim Klavierspiel* (The doctrine of unified art of piano playing) (Berlin: Raabe & Plothow, 1885).

13. Undoubtedly based upon the symbolic meaning of the number 3 in the Catholic religion.

14. *Brahms' Noblesse*, 277.

15. "Fruchtbarkeit aus innerer Notwendigkeit," *Liszts Offenbarung*, 57.

16. *Liszts Offenbarung*, 45.

17. Plotinus, *The Enneads*, 1.6.2. and 5.8.1, as quoted in Rowell, 87.

18. "The hidden harmony is better than the obvious." Heraclitus, *Fragments*, 116, as quoted in Rowell, 43. Leibniz's Monad no. 81 (see Chapter 3: 47) is another example of Clark's perception of harmony.

19. In German: "Moderierung."

20. *Das Musizieren der Zukunft*, Vol. 1 No. 4 (March 1908), 260.

21. "The Physical Cause of Harmony and Disharmony," Naturforscherversammlung (Natural Research Conference) in Karlsruhe, September 1858.

22. Friedrich Jacob Kurt Geißler, *Eine mögliche Wesenerklärung für Raum, Zeit, das Unendliche und die Kausalität, nebst einem Grundwort zur Metaphysik der Möglichkeiten* (Berlin: Gutenberg, 1900).

23. Isidor de Seville, *Etymologiarum sive originum libri xx*, 3.15-23, as translated in Oliver Strunk, *Source Readings in Music History* (New York: Norton, 1950), 94, 100.

24. As quoted in Rowell, 79.

25. *Das Musizieren der Zukunft*, Vol. 1 No. 4 (March 1908), 267.

26. *Brahms' Noblesse*, 9.

27. *Liber de sumo bono*, 2. tr. 3, c. 5, as quoted in Rowell, 93.

28. *Liszts Offenbarung*, 238: "Wirbelproportionierung kinematischer Freiheit." Also, 174: "Only the proportional oscillation . . . allows a challenging, universal action of all members from the heart to the hands, and naturally of any spiritual possession." (Allein die Wirbelproportionierung, . . . erlaubt ein herausforderndes, allseitiges Wirken jedes Gliedes vom Herzen bis zu den Händen und natürlich auch jedes geistige Vermögen).

29. As quoted in *Das Musizieren*, Vol. 1 No. 4 (January 1909), 295. This quote sounds quite credible, given Bismarck's historical mission, while probably referring to a much more general context than that used by Clark. It is also confirmed by the remark in *Iphigenia* (see chapter 1, note 25,

5

The New Technique

The following description of the principles of Clark's technique is an attempt to formulate an "ultimate" version, resulting from combining his early and late works. Although *Die Lehre des einheitlichen Kunstmittels beim Klavierspiel*[1] is based on a conventional keyboard, and *Brahms' Noblesse*[2] and *Pianistenharmonie*[3] on either an elevated model or a two-keyboard system, there is no doubt that all these works by Clark are based upon an early-formed set of principles which were just abridged, renamed, and reapplied in the late version.

As mentioned in chapter 3, in the preface of *Die Lehre*, Clark, signed as "Frederic Clark-Steiniger," expressed his gratitude, among others, to Hermann Helmholtz, who apparently had written Clark a short note expressing dissatisfaction with the lack of variety in executing different touches on the piano. Helmholtz wrote: "As far as I see it, new (piano) mechanisms allow only a change of speed with which the hammer attacks the string, i.e., of the force of attack on the key."[4] In coping with this problem, Clark was inspired by the belief that nature provides mankind with means to interpret and realize the laws that allow material manifestations of our thoughts. His human and artistic credo is expressed in the following thought: "In order to subordinate execution and technique to the artistic ideas, we have to choose the form of power and movement which absolutely mirrors a continuous and progressive flow of thoughts."[5] Clark therefore regarded the body as a part of the complex unit it creates with the piano, and stressed the importance of perceiving the continuity of the muscle action during and between playing notes.

The first occasion on which he realized there is something beyond finger action was in November 1877, when a German student of Dr. Oscar Paul (his own teacher) played Chopin's first Scherzo in a way that was like "a veritable whirlwind so volicitious, and yet like a hailstorm, so definite were the tones. They were not hit by separate strokes of fingers but they were included as like leaves hurled about in the vortices of the driving storm."[6] From this experience he coined the term "vital touch," which he witnessed only once afterward, when listening "within hand's reach" to Clara Schumann in the Berlin Singakademie in February 1883. Clark later maintained that Paul was the only teacher in Leipzig who did not give classical finger exercises or asked for highly-lifted fingers (on the contrary, he demanded listening to the sound throughout its duration and connecting it seamlessly with the next one), and that he eventually quit his position in reaction to well-entrenched methods. Also, Paul emphasized that a pianist should be an athlete and often took Clark with him to his swimming and gymnastic exercises. However, by far the strongest influence against isolated finger work came from a Jakob Hahn, one of Plaidy's[7] last students, who was also a student of the conservatory in Leipzig and founded the Detroit Conservatory in 1872.

In *Die Lehre*, Clark dedicated a whole chapter to the description of physiological facts and recommended posture and action at the keyboard. He drew the conclusions from a set of mathematical-physical formulas describing the properties and the interaction of the parts of the playing apparatus. These formulas, appearing to be too scientific and innovative for the "art-teachers," were subject to ridicule. Describing in great detail the anatomical structure of the playing mechanism, Clark also suggested exercises to train the muscles involved in the process of playing, organizing them by the groups that perform together, and warning against protracted periods of tension during exercise. He also considered the elasticity of shoulder muscles and shoulder blades of utmost importance to natural, relaxed, and controlled tone production. He saw relaxed and loose shoulders as a consequence of a straight and actively supported spine. An approximate 45 degree decline of the upper arm from the torso assured that the hand could reach the extremes of the keyboard without back movement. This angle, somewhat larger than is customarily applied, suggests that sitting farther away from the keyboard, and possibly lower, could be more advantageous.[8] His final standing position is but an extreme consequence of this reasoning.

Following the old Greek adage *mens sana in corpora sano* (a healthy mind in a healthy body), Clark reminded that neglecting either at the expense of the other leads to an imbalanced expression. He wrote:

> To create the absolute unity of the body and the spirit which is necessary for the expression of an idea in the reproductive art, to create conscious life in physical detail in order to develop psycho-physical consciousness, to observe the natural laws to which a body must conform, and to perform all of it as a momentary act of the will, all of this makes possible the factual confirmation of the unification of the study of arts and the cultivation of character, so far believed to be unattainable.[9]

Demanding the use of *phorolyse*[10] as a basic procedure in playing, Clark complained that the other methods concentrated solely on the moment of tone production. Clark's criticism of other piano methods continued with the fact that all of them are concerned with only a part (finger, hand, or forearm) of the tone-building process, never attempting to build a unified system. Clark asserted that an organic system of masses (human body), being moved by an uninterrupted flow of energy, satisfies the elementary requirements of technique. A system of masses that can constantly maintain the level of energy, producing as much as it spends, would be approximating the action of a *perpetuum mobile*. Such a system would also satisfy the requirements of an economical performance. If one succeeds in combining the two actions, while exercising full mental understanding and control of the process, the will is able to transform the images of the spirit directly into a continuing, purposeful image. Therefore, concluded Clark, all unilateral and linear movements are selective, and restrict the complete development of the system. Accordingly, all methods that insist upon isolated actions and linear movements, both of which obstruct the conjunction of organic forces, must be wrong. Clark was convinced that the sound had to occur as an imminent consequence of the movement, which in turn had to mediate a true picture of the logical sequence of thoughts in a musical work. Even if this chain worked perfectly, Clark regarded the resulting music only as a casual by-product of the original harmonic activity that permeates playing. This activity he considered to be the definitive manifestation of love for God.

Clark felt the contradiction between the broken movements of a pianist's arms and the continuous motion of music. His model for avoiding this contradiction was, as shown, the motion of the earth around its axis and the sun, combined with rotation of the sun around the weight-center of the solar system, which in turn moves forward in a straight line.

When applied to the pianist, Clark saw that this rotating system describes an oval cylinder, with a shape not unlike a bowling pin. The power of tone production and the movements for the duration of the sound were to be regulated with the elasticity of torsion along the shoulder-finger axis. The general origin and coordination of the movements was in the solar plexus. Clark conceived the chain of motion transfer starting with groups of large muscles, which are easiest to control. The rotating momentum of vibrating impulses from the shoulder blades are thus transferred to smaller and smaller units, which are more difficult to control but easier to move quickly. If any part of the arm would be lifted or dropped in an isolated motion, the form of the movement would have been changed, and the self-enclosed system suggested by Clark would no longer function. To play a succession of tones, as in a scale, it is necessary to incorporate such rotating units into a system. The resulting ratio of movements, generally also corresponding to the periodic or phrasing structure in music is, as mentioned in chapter 4, 1 elliptic torso motion (an eight-measure period) : 2 rotary arm motions : 4 double-curve forearm motions : 8 or 16 epi-cycloidal hand motions (motives or shortest musical units).

This is supposedly how Liszt described the action of such a system, quoted from or attributed to Liszt by Clark in the book *Liszts Offenbarung*:

> The inner members, such as forearm and upper arm, are more subject to the curve of the articulation than the hand, which lies at the periphery. Even as the forearm, fulfilling its function and forming a phrase, turns inwards and downwards in pronation and then outwards und upwards in supination, describing a double curve, so does the hand at the same time make several vibrating rotations, being induced in cycloid forms through the larger circles of the upper arm, which control it.[11]

Clark illustrated this harmonic connection as shown below.

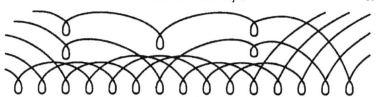

Figure 5.1. An illustration of proportions in a rotating system,
after Figure 8 in *Die Lehre*.

A review of Clark's 1911 concert provides another graphic illustration:
"The arms described self-enclosed circles corresponding to musical
phrases, the hand-shells turned now in now out, reaching into the keys
and the retreating. Even the slow passages were divided in similar,
self-enclosed movements."[12] In his book *Die natürliche Klavier-
technik*,[13] Rudolf Maria Breithaupt points to the fact that this graphic
fixation of rolling movements, *Rollungen*, as Breithaupt called them, is
positively the first in the history of piano technique. Rotation and
torsion are integral parts of Clark's system, and they were, according
to him, possible in all parts of the system. He saw the variability of the
torque along the spine-finger axis as the regulator of the power of tone
production and of the movements for the duration of the sound. Here
Clark called again on Helmholtz, who, as Clark related, had recently
proved that fingers could participate in torsion.[14] This statement,
however, was challenged by Breithaupt, who criticized Clark's demand
for rotation and dynamic tension in all joints. Breithaupt considered
that forearm and arm rotation were confused with arm turn, and that
the rotation axes could be considered only through wrist points. Thus,
one may conclude that Breithaupt considered the fingers only as an
appendix to the elbow-wrist axis. Clark's system offered a potentially
more refined control of the fingers, since their tips were also used as
rotation points.

The ultimate goal of Clark's detailed technical descriptions was to
unify and coordinate the interaction of the human mind and body with
the piano. Clark noticed that similar goals and notions might already
have resided in the subconsciousness of some ingenious minds, such as
Liszt, Rubinstein, and d'Albert. Nevertheless, this coordination and
the required technical skills could without any doubt be assimilated by
anyone willing to learn and understand them. Clark warned that such
an accomplishment would not cause or guarantee in any manner an
improvement of interpretative capabilities *per se*.

Clark spent ten years in research and study of the whole problem. During this time his belief in his teachers and widely accepted methods grew weaker, and gradually became replaced by his own logical judgment and study of physiological facts. When *Die Lehre* was published, it was probably the reaction of the authors of fashionable methods and of teachers that made his publication forgotten right away. The only other author, apart from Steinhausen, who recognized the value of new ideas in Clark's book is again Breithaupt, who, albeit only in the third edition of his book *Die natürliche Klaviertechnik*, writes:

> The founder of the *physiological school* of our technique, and especially the *shoulder mechanics* is not Ludwig Deppe, but, according to newer research, it is beyond doubt Horace Frederick [*sic*] Clark. (See his work *Die Lehre des einheitlichen Kunstmittels beim Klavierspiel*, Berlin 1885, in which the unity of the organic system of masses, the cyclic forms of motion ['Rollungen'], and the *pulling down* of the shoulder-blade [p. 46] are already completely represented.) This also supersedes the priority of E[lisabeth]. Caland. According to competent judgments of older students of Deppe, like T. Bandmann, Frau Prof. Döring - Coburg, music director Klose - Hanover, and others, being also his occasional student, she is more of a immediate follower and perpetuator of Clark's ideas.[15]

However, in an earlier (second) edition of his book, Breithaupt stated that "the doctrine of unity of 1885 is worth attention ONLY in the part about stressing the freedom, especially of the shoulder, as well as his preference of the pronation position."[16] The only full entry under his own name that Clark received is in the modern encyclopedia *Die Musik in der Geschichte und Gegenwart*.[17] The description by Kurt Johnen is relatively concise. He appeared satisfied by confirming Clark's priority in applying some "new conclusions, which only later became publicly recognized." Johnen also mentions Clark's request for an uninterrupted movement sequence, and his poetic graphical organization of musical works.

With the new conclusions and demands in *Die Lehre*, Clark made the case for the need for a conscious and scientific understanding of the pianist's body, requiring full conformity with axioms such as the unity of body and soul, and the observation of nature's laws. The former later became the microcosmic relationship in his *Harmonie*, while the latter transformed into "Creator's laws," and the macrocosmic relationship.

Clark was very much aware of the fact that the progressive ideas he carried would need a considerable amount of time to overcome resistance and to find a fertile musical soil. Clark himself might have as well uttered the sentence that he ascribes to Liszt: ". . . and I am convinced that it will be at least the year 1940 before the musical world realizes and learns what classicity in piano playing means."[18]

Fortunately, at least the physiological facts on which Clark based his method have been corroborated before then, in 1929. Otto Ortmann's book *The Physiological Mechanics of Piano Technique*[19] is still the most valuable source for the understanding of a pianist's playing apparatus. Ortmann criticized the limitations of the regular keyboard,[20] and criticized most of the methods of its usage, including Breithaupt, who had criticized Clark. Ortmann mentions the usage of the vertical movement of the shoulder girdle in playing fortissimo chords, the movement which, as mentioned above, Breithaupt attributed to Clark and called it a "pulling down" of the shoulder blades.[21] Ortmann also dismisses all schools preaching isolated movements, since practically all the movements are of a complex nature, and the source of the movement is never in the joint that is actually moving.[22] He writes: "The whole neural system is opposed to isolated or disintegrated action. . . . Piano technique, for its adequate acquisition, demands a coordination. . . ."[23] This emphasizes Clark's insistence upon the spine (solar plexus region) as the source of the general coordination, because it, accordingly, allows movements in all the joints along the axis.

Ortmann attacks rectilinear movements for their lack of freedom and awkwardness. He also points out that percussiveness interferes with the efficiency of weight transfer, a problem that Clark's method has effectively eliminated, both on a regular and on an inclined keyboard (see chapter 6). Clark foresaw the problem that Ortmann noticed, namely that even in an apparent state of relaxation the hand still maintains some finger flexion to grasp the keys. Clark's inclined keyboard and concave key-caps eliminate the necessity for such static tension almost completely.

The lateral arm movement, shown in its perfect coordinated form in Ortmann as an inverted-eight figure,[24] corresponds completely to the double-curve description of Clark's coordinated movement. Although it may seem that Ortmann opposes the rolling movement *(Rollbewegung)*, which in other terms undoubtedly exists in Clark's technique, it is the weight transfer during the ascent that Ortmann is opposed to, since that movement would be uncoordinated and wasteful. The photographs in Ortmann showing the hand movement in a scale and an arpeggio execution[25] are almost identical to the diagrams Clark drew without the benefit of (then) sophisticated equipment. Those drawings of rolling movements, recognized by Breithaupt, show how accurate and understanding were Clark's eyes. Ingenious and effective, though not sophisticated, Ortmann's equipment and his tests provided substantial corroborating evidence to support Clark's early ideas. Although this validation came too late for Clark, it dispels any doubt as to the validity and accuracy of Clark's basic premises.

Notes

1. (Berlin: Raabe & Plothow, 1885).
2. (Zürich: Pianistenharmoniepresse, 1914).
3. (Berlin: n.p., 1910).
4. In the original: "Soweit ich sehe, kann bei den neueren Mechanismen nur der Geschwindigkeitsgrad, mit welchem der Hammer gegen die Saite fliegt, d. h. die Kraft des Anschlags von der Taste aus modificirt werden." (*Die Lehre*, 4)
5. *Die Lehre*, 8.
6. *Music of the Future and of the Present* Vol. 1 No. 3 (December 1901): 178.
7. Louis Plaidy (1810-1874) was a famous German piano teacher who began his professional career as a violinist. He took piano lessons from Agthe (the same teacher Anna Steiniger studied with) and in 1843 was engaged by Mendelssohn as a piano teacher at the Leipzig Conservatory, where he taught until 1865.
8. The advantages of low sitting apparently first came to his attention while observing Clara Schumann at her 1876 Gewandhaus concert.
9. *Die Lehre*, 49:

> Die absolute Einheit des Körpers und Geistes nothwendig für den Ausdruck eines Gedankens in der reproducirenden Kunst, die Erzeugung bewussten Lebens in physischen details zur Entwicklung des psycho-psysischen Bewusstseins, die Beobachtung der Naturgesetze, denen das Organ sich unterordnen muss, und schliesslich die Übersicht des Verstandes, dieses Alles zu einer momentanen Handlung des Willens zu machen, ermöglicht die bisher geglaubte unerreichbare Feststellung [der Vereinigung—added in handwriting, quite possibly by the author himself; if the

original would have only '. . . Festellung zwischen . . .' it could be translated as 'the connection between'] zwischen Kunststudium und Charakterbildung.

10. This term was also an object of ridicule in Dorn's review. The term itself was described in *Liszts Offenbarung: Schlüssel zur Freiheit des Individuums* (Berlin: C. F. Vieweg, 1907), 301, as the analysis of motion and criticism of methods.

11. *Liszts Offenbarung*, 51:

> Die Innenglieder, zum Beispiel Vorderarm und Oberarm, sind mehr auf die Kurve der Artikulation angewiesen als die äußere an der Peripherie liegende Hand. Und wie der Vorderarm, um seine Funktion zu vollziehen und die Kola zu gestalten, in Pronation nach innen und unten sich dreht, danach in Supination nach oben und außen abwechselt in Doppelkurven, muß zu gleicher Zeit die Hand vielmals wirbelnd rotieren, hineingeführt in Zykloide durch das sie bestimmende größere Kreisen des Oberarms.

12. A review by a "Dr. of philosophy" of the concert Clark gave on 30 October 1911 in Jena, on the occasion of Liszt's 100th birthday, as quoted in *Das Musizieren der Zukunft*, Vol. 2 No. 1 (March 1912): 343.

13. (Leipzig: C. F. Kahnt Nachfolger, 1912; 1st ed., 1905), 225. Breithaupt asserts that Clark was the first to discuss the possibility of pulling the shoulder blade down. From Breithaupt's syntax it results that Clark was the one to recommend this approach for playing fast, usually repeated, series of octaves and chords. Breithaupt immediately warned against the exaggeration in such an approach. Clark, however, only listed this movement in a batch of exercises related to the shoulder girdle (*Die Lehre*, 46). Breithaupt also mentions that Elisabeth Caland has described this aid procedure better and in more detail. This appears to be a corroboration of Clark's statement that Caland has stolen, misinterpreted, and warped his original ideas.

14. *Die Lehre*, 12.

15. *Klaviertechnik*, vii (the square brackets within the parenthetical sentence are Breithaupt's):

> Der Begründer der *physiologischen Richtung* unserer Kunsttechnik, sowie vor allem der *Schulter-Mechanik*, ist nach neuren Forschungen *nicht* Ludwig Deppe, sondern zweifels- ohne *Horace Frederick Clark*. (Vergl. dessen Schrift: *Die Lehre des einheitlichen Kunstmittels beim Klavierspiel*, Berlin 1885, in der schon die Einheitlichkeit des organischen Massensystems sowie die cyklischen Bewegungsformen ['Rollungen'] und das '*Nach-Unten-Ziehen*' des

Schulterblattes [pag. 46] genau dargestellt sind.) Damit fällt
auch die priorität E. Calands in sich zusammen. E. Caland ist
vielmehr nach kompetenten Urteilen älterer Deppe-Schüler wie
T. Bandmann, Frau Prof. Döring - Coburg, Musikdirektor
Klose - Hannover u. a., die unmittelbare Nachfolgerin und
Fortsetzerin der Ideen H. F. Clarks, dessen Schülerin sie auch
zeitweise war.

16. *Klaviertechnik*, 2nd edition, 366, as quoted in *Das Musizieren der
Zukunft*, Vol. 1 No. 4 (July 1908), 280. This remark was part of a chapter
Breithaupt entitled "Unnatural Piano Technique!"

17. "Die von ihm vertretenen neuen kl[avier].-pädagogischen Ideen
nehmen eine Reihe von Erkenntnissen vorweg, die erst durch spätere
Forschungen unabhängig von ihm Allgemeingut wurden."

18. *Liszts Offenbarung*, 103: ". . . und ich bin überzeugt, bevor die
musikalische Welt erkennen und wissen wird, was Klassizität im Klavierspiel
bedeutet, wird man mindestens schon im Jahre 1940 sein."

19. (New York: E. P. Dutton, 1962, paperback).

20. See chapter 6, p. 82.

21. Ortmann, 19.

22. Ortmann, 39.

23. Ortmann, 71.

24. Ortmann, 163ff.

25. Ortmann, facing pp. 256 and 266.

6

The Harmonie-*piano: "Soul-Mirror"*

It is very difficult to find the exact source for Clark's concept of the *Harmonie*-piano. Although he ascribed the idea and the first experiments to Johannes Brahms in his book *Brahms' Noblesse*,[1] Clark's statement to that effect, in the light of the other dubious assumptions made in the book, is not very convincing. Moreover, there is no mention even of the idea in *Die Lehre des einheitlichen Kunstmittels*, published at least ten years after Clark's meeting with Brahms took place.[2] The episode with Brahms, on the other hand, waited for almost forty years before it was described in *Brahms' Noblesse*.

The earliest mention of a new instrument, as a result of a new method, comes from *Liszts Offenbarung*,[3] where Liszt supposedly states:

> It will take a fundamentally different theory and practice of the piano technique, based on arch construction and vibrating systems of the free will; it will take a different piano, not percussive, but built on sideways motion,[4] or even built of endless ball-joints; it will take an artist who feels the *Harmonie* in himself and wants to bring it out; it will take an audience, which will understand the *Harmonie* and will want to listen to it—it will take all of these and still other prerequisites before a man will be able to call this art of the future great, or true, or beautiful.[5]

In trying to reconstruct the probable true historic sequence of events, it seems that the most logical place to start is the alleged revelation Clark had in 1885. The stipulation that Clark had a vision becomes quite credible if one thinks of the extent his life was immersed into religion and philosophy—corroborated by the reports of Bettina Walker, W. S. B. Mathews, and Clark's own writings.

The most obvious source of doubt regarding the factual accuracy in *Brahms' Noblesse* arises from his description of the revelation in this book. In the appendix, entitled "Second Letter to Emperor Wilhelm II, about the *Harmonie*," Clark asserts that the idea of the double-keyboard piano as the soul-mirror was one of the main events in his revelation. It was supposedly only on the advice of his friends that he refrained from publishing the idea about the piano; he came out only with a different technical approach. In the text of *Brahms' Noblesse*, however, Clark claims that he saw the first experimental version of the piano when he was talking to Brahms in 1876, and he includes the photograph of himself (not Brahms!) at the experimental keyboards, calling it "Brahms developing the golden-mean-keyboards."[6] Brahms also supposedly asked him not to mention any idea of this experiment and its benefits to the world until after Brahms's death.[7]

If this is true, then Clark certainly held to his word, having published the discovery only in 1914, and, according to reviews in the same book, having played publicly on *his* perfected model of the *Harmonie*-piano since (at least) 1911. But the illustrations from the book *Pianistenharmonie* (1910) show one, not two, elevated keyboards, whereas all the illustrations in *Brahms' Noblesse* show a two-keyboard system, to be played in a "crucifix" or "cherubim" position. According to one of the pictures in *Pianistenharmonie* the piano was manufactured by ". . .yford Bros." [beginning of first name illegible], and patented on 21 January 1908 in Syracuse, New York. The caption states it is a "D. R. Patent," but Clark certainly must have been referring to his keyboard patent (see below) rather than to the piano as a whole. There is no reference to the number of keyboards in the patent itself.

The two-keyboard system appears to have been built only in 1913 by "W. Steuer in Berlin,"[8] and Clark claimed in a letter to Wilhelm II that it was the first experimental model.[9] In a further photograph in *Brahms' Noblesse* (see photo of Clark at the piano), Clark claims the first public introduction of this system, in Zurich, and in the same year (1913). This means that he had somehow transported the whole system to Switzerland. It is confusing, though, that the photographs mentioning Steuer in Berlin and the public introduction in Zurich were obviously taken at the same place. The only explanation could be that he made these photographs after he had moved, simply wanting to credit the manufacturer. This does not answer why he needed separate photographs to accomplish his goal. Perhaps the same kind of naiveté like the one already mentioned, with Clark in the photograph presented as Brahms in the legend, is involved.

The only plausible explanation of all these controversies is that Clark probably had the idea himself—whether already in 1885 or some later time is impossible to confirm.[10] Clark claims it took him twenty-five years to perfect the final version. It is possible that, confronted with the lack of means, he first had a two-keyboard experimental model, then a one-keyboard performing model, and finally the two-keyboard system built at the time of publication of *Brahms' Noblesse*. From his various writings one can deduct that he made some experiments with playing in standing position, for several months, after his "revelation" in 1885. At that time the keyboard was at the height of a hanging elbow. In 1887 in Boston he brought the keyboard again to normal position, no doubt pressured by the reaction to the "Clark-Steiniger" method. This, however, he bitterly regretted, stating later that he lost twenty years of development by yielding to pressure.

The Royal German Patent Number 225,637 is dated 23 October 1909. According to the accompanying text, it was conceived to eliminate the curving and hammer-like activity of the longer fingers, and thus favor and facilitate a "caressing" rather than "beating" touch. The device itself enables the elements of the tone-producing mechanism in a piano (hammer, damper, key) to return to their initial position even from an inclined position (see drawing), the whole keyboard being totally detachable. Its inclination was adjustable.[11] Under the keys are springs to preserve the original key-resistance in this inclination. This is all that can be deduced from the patent; the remainder of the following description is found in *Brahms' Noblesse*.[12] The keyboard is elevated to shoulder level. The caps (faces) of the keys are slightly curved (concave), to allow the fingers to cling better. The inclination actually makes the thumb play more with its flat side, and certainly puts it closer and more even in respect to the other fingers.[13] The pianist stands in front (later probably between two keyboards) with outstretched arms, thus eliminating all angles and establishing a general axis from the fingertips to the solar plexus, through the arms, shoulders, and spine. From the picture of the two-keyboard system it seems that the pianist would move between the keyboards, using three pairs of pedals that he could step on as he moved to and fro. It is not clear whether the keyboards themselves were mirroring each other, as the name "soul-mirror" might suggest—if so, one of the keyboards had to have a reverse order of strings and keys!

Re-creating with this "Cherubim-doctrine" the old Greek principle of the "golden-mean," Clark thought that through this posture he had blended all extensors and flexors into one unbroken vortex-like motion, avoiding any angularity and detached motions. This piano falls into the experimental keyboard category, joining the designs of Lunn, Janko, Moór, Wieniawski, Mangeot, Clutsam, Staufer, and Heidinger.[14] For various reasons, few of them have survived the phase of experimental models. Although Clark received some positive reactions, German tradition was too conservative for innovations such as playing the piano from a standing position.

A pianist playing in such an unusual stance would also encounter some problems. The most obvious one is visual coordination. Common sense would suggest that playing an intricate piece without a combination of stereovision, as we have it, and hemispheric vision such as found, for example, in frogs, would be very difficult. It is impossible, though, to perceive the benefits and the influence of a concentrated and unified system of mind and body on that problem without extensive practical research.

The next question concerns the amount of physical endurance required to hold one's arms above the shoulder level. Although the position is maintained through active muscular effort (meaning alternation of tension and release), there always must be present a certain required minimum of tension in order to retain the position even during, relatively speaking, relaxation periods. The customary sitting position, with the arms below shoulder level, certainly offers less resistance to the omnipresent gravity. However, from the battery of physical exercises he suggested, and from the importance he placed on equal development of mind and body, it is obvious that Clark did not regard piano playing as a leisurely enterprise. Moreover, he insists that by presenting a problem of the highest difficulty and complexity for the human will he has created a way of attaining the highest and most ennobled form of art.[15]

There is also the problem of total body coordination during playing. Clark never once mentioned in his books the body below the waist, with the exception of his very first book. In *Die Lehre*, which anyway refers to the ordinary sitting position, he stressed the importance of the legs' support for the freedom of the torso. Apparently he did not consider the legs as having any active part in his bodily solar system duplication, although one may assume that he preferred the standing position simply in order to prevent *any* extremity from assuming an angular position. Keeping balance while moving between the two keyboards is probably not an easy task. In addition, it was also possibly necessary to rotate the torso, depending upon the placement and order of strings, which cannot be verified. Coordinating such a complicated sequence of movements, while trying to reach and maintain pressure on the pedal, would be quite difficult. If, in addition to that, one had to move and switch to the next pair of pedals (the photograph shows three pairs), the transition was certainly cumbersome. Furthermore, if it were necessary to use half-pedal, or vibrating pedal, exerting a controlled light pressure on the pedal while moving over it with the body would be next to impossible. Clark, however, already encountered such criticisms and rebutted them with indignation saying that, on the contrary, the pedal action was "refreshingly light" in comparison with the regular one and the criticisms came from those who never experimented with the action.[16]

Finally, it is difficult to judge acoustical properties of what amounts to two vertical pianos projecting their sound in two diametrically opposite directions. Although there is no mention of the positioning on stage, it is likely that Clark played it as an organist would, turned with his back toward the audience, which would mean that the sound reached the listeners only indirectly and, perhaps, with questionable quality. However, since Clark mentioned that there were sixteen hundred present at his Jena concert, and no mention was made in the reviews about acoustical deficiencies, the sound must have been satisfactory to a degree.

Clark claimed he himself needed several years before he was able to apply totally his 1885 method, which he later enriched with the implementation of proportional rotations of the segments of the playing mechanism, even on very simple pieces. This was, however, still in the traditional sitting position. Adding to this the complications of coordination, movements of the body (probably even backward), and pedaling, it is very doubtful that any human being, even an accomplished gymnast-turned-pianist, could attain the necessary perfection in coordination, and in addition contemplate and realize a total *freedom* of action along with a unity between the mind and the body, microcosm and macrocosm, individual and universal, and earthly and divine. It would be the sort of effort that only somebody with extensive training in body- and mind-controlling techniques (yoga, Zen, t'ai chi, some martial arts) could hope to accomplish. It is true, therefore, that such an accomplishment would bring the "harmonizer" (the term Clark used to describe himself) to a mental state which, for lack of a better expression, one could describe as "nirvana" or "absolute peace and unity with the world," or "linking the divine and the human." "Iphigenia" says:

> Every book on pianoforte playing has regarded the keyboard as an arbitrary tyrant. St. Damian [Clark's pseudonym] was the first who said: "Unity-absolute shall absorb the entire being—mind, emotion, body, of the pianist; and this living harmony of intelligent force, shall be pronounced upon the pianoforte, shall efform ideal tone-effects without compromise to the manual characteristics of the instrument; *for what is right, and what is ideal law or harmony in the soul and body of the artist, will and shall be, nay is, and that only is, right in the action of his art!*"[17] [original italics]

What should certainly be remembered from this experiment is the attempt to relate the axes and planes of the playing surface and the playing mechanism. In his book *The Physiological Mechanics of Piano Technique*,[18] Otto Ortmann addresses matter-of-factly the limitations of the standard keyboard. He notices that piano technique has adapted itself to the form of the keyboard, and that the keyboard's most obvious drawback is the limitation of the forward armshift, imposed by the fallboard. He suggests moving the fallboard a few inches back, thus allowing curvilinear, instead of simply linear, motions.[19] Angular movement on a standard keyboard requires more muscular strength and higher coordination, and increases the inhibition by restraining forward movement. Thus, a curvilinear keyboard, such as Staufer's and Heidinger's (1824) or Clutsam's (1907), or one without the fallboard such as Clark's, would be much more economical. Ortmann also mentions a "duplex type" keyboard,[20] but it is not clear whether he was aware of, or was aiming at, Clark's keyboard. The only book of Clark mentioned by Ortmann in an appendix is *Die Lehre*, which does not yet have any mention of an inclined keyboard or a two-keyboard system.

The idea of curving the key caps is also interesting. Clark is not very explicit on how they were curved (back-to-front, or also laterally). In only one instance he mentions "crescent-capped" keys.[21] This change would probably close even more the angle between the arms' and keyboard's axes.

Contemplating the whole evolution of Clark's technical principles and their practical implementation, and speculating on their possibilities, it seems that he consciously chose to overlook one possible interim model which would combine a traditional but modern physiological approach, such as introduced in *Die Lehre*, with the improved keyboard: an inclined keyboard, or even a two-keyboard system, which could be played from a sitting position. His inability to compromise in his undertaking probably led him to ignore the most obvious practical advantage of such a system—a free lower body, which would enable much easier pedaling and also provide stronger support to the torso, regardless of the position. The upper body could function as a centralized system, while eliminating all superfluous angles, and thus still be in accord with Clark's original physiologically unifying principles.

Notes

1. (Zürich: Pianistenharmoniepresse, 1914), 141. Brahms allegedly realized the additional freedom and easiness in playing while stretching his arms to reach the second and third manuals on a church organ.

2. (Berlin: Raabe & Plothow, 1885).

3. Clark, *Liszts Offenbarung: Schlüssel zur Freiheit des Individuums* (Berlin: C. F. Vieweg, 1907).

4. In the original, "Bebung." Here Clark uses an unfortunate technical term associated with the clavichord. What he means is probably a side attack rather than a frontal attack.

5. *Liszts Offenbarung*, 52:

> Eine von Grund aus verschiedene, auf Bogensehnen und Wirbelsystemen des freien Willens beruhende Techniktheorie und -Praxis; ein anderes Klavier, nicht schlagartig, sondern auf Bebung gebaut, sogar unendlich kugellenkig; ein Künstler, der die Harmonie in sich fühlt und zum Ausdruck zu bringen vermag; ein Publikum, das die Harmonie versteht und ihr lauschen möchte – alles das und noch andere Vorbedingungen gehören dazu, ehe man diese größte Kunst der Zukunft groß oder wahr oder schön heißen kann.

6. *Brahms' Noblesse*, 32: "Brahms Ausprobierung Goldene-Mitte-Klaviaturen."

7. Similarly, Liszt supposedly asked him to work secretly for thirty years on perfecting his approach, before revealing it. (*Liszts Offenbarung*, 213).

8. *Brahms' Noblesse*, after page 224. The company was founded by Wilhelm Steuer in Berlin, in 1894.

9. *Brahms' Noblesse*, 429. Clark was probably referring to the two-keyboard model.

10. In *Das Musizieren* Vol. 1 No. 4 (March 1908), 256, he claimed that he finally summoned the courage on 15 August 1907 (the day Joseph Joachim died, as Clark adds correctly) to lift the piano onto his writing desk.

11. In the final version of Clark's piano perhaps as much as 66 degrees. It was apparently offered by a professor of music at the Jena University, as a result of Clark's successful 1911 Jena concert (Liszt anniversary) and it was "3/4 inclined."

12. *Brahms' Noblesse*, 135. It is probable that the alterations described here by Brahms were actually undertaken by Clark for the last model of his piano, a gift by the aforementioned professor, which would also account for the fact that the official inauguration date Clark puts on it is 1913, two years after it was promised.

13. *Brahms' Noblesse*, 367. Clark, speaking through Brahms, describes the advantage thus:

> The most velocituous studies, as for example this C-sharp minor etude of Chopin I can play more rapidly, distinctly, and powerfully than the "really" great pianists, for I do not, like them, have to make farther way to the keys with my thumb than with the long fingers. Thus all my fingers and thumb also lie in the general path of extension, immediately over the keys, so that the most minimal cycloidal impulse of the hand from out of the elbow and armpit, creates the tones of the motive and phrase.

14. Nicolas Meeus, "Keyboard," *The New Grove Dictionary of Music and Musicians* (1980).

15. *Das Musizieren der Zukunft*, Vol. 1 No. 4 (December 1907), 232.

16. *Das Musizieren der Zukunft*, Vol. 1 No. 4 (December 1907), 232.

17. *Iphigenia*, 247.

18. (New York: E. P. Dutton, 1962, paperback).

19. Ortmann, 280-82.

20. Ortmann, 280.

21. *Brahms' Noblesse*, 281.

Frederic Horace Clark at an early model of one-keyboard
elevated piano with an inclined keyboard

Anna Steiniger

Die

2680 6

Lehre des einheitlichen Kunstmittels

beim Clavierspiel.

Eine Kritik der Claviermethoden.

Von

Frederic Clark-Steiniger.

Mit 24 Abbildungen.

Berlin.

Verlag von Raabe & Plothow.
Potsdamer Strasse Nr. 9.

Front page of Clark's first book
Die Lehre des einheitlichen Kunstmittels

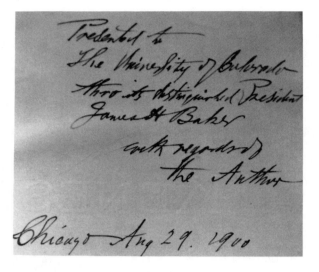

Clark's dedication of a copy of *Die Lehre*

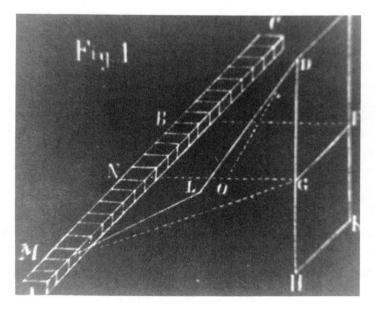

Figure 1 in *Die Lehre*, demonstrating the geometrical
proportions of the playing mechanism

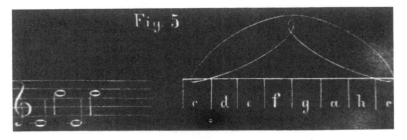

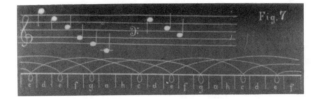

Figure 5 in *Die Lehre*, demonstrating one of basic
compound movements

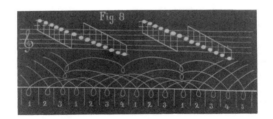

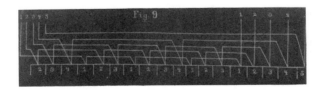

Figures 7-9 in *Die Lehre*, showing an increasing degree of
complexity in coordination of arpeggios and scales

KAISERLICHES PATENTAMT

PATENTSCHRIFT

№ 225637

KLASSE 51*h*. GRUPPE 20.

FREDERIC HORAZ CLARK in HALENSEE b. BERLIN.

Klaviatur für Pianos.

Patentiert im Deutschen Reiche vom 23. Oktober 1909 ab.

Die Tasten des Klaviers in horizontaler Fläche liegen für die kurzen Finger (Daumen und kleinen Finger) passend, jedoch für die längeren Finger derart, daß sie eine Krümmung und Hammertätigkeit letzterer beanspruchen.

Um einen besseren, mehr streichenden als klopfenden Anschlag zu erzielen, soll nach vorliegender Erfindung der Klaviatur eine geneigte, und zwar beliebig einstellbare Lage gegeben werden.

Nach Fig. 1 ist die Pianomechanik a mit der Taste b mittels eines senkrechten, geraden Gliedes a, b verbunden. Dieses neue Glied a, b ist an beiden Enden mit Gelenk versehen und kann eine beliebige Länge haben. Das Tastenbrett c ist um Zapfen d drehbar, die genau in der Richtung der Gelenke b_1 liegen, und läßt sich mittels Stifte e beliebig feststellen, so daß die Tastatur mehr oder weniger schräg oder auch horizontal oder aber, wenn nicht in Gebrauch, nach unten völlig zurückgelegt werden kann.

Nach Fig. 2 ist dieselbe Wirkung mittels eines horizontal zwischen Taste b und Mechanik c eingeschobenen Gliedes a erreicht, das an eine Leiste d unter Zwischenschaltung eines Gelenkstückes f oder auch mittels eines einzelnen Gelenkes angehängt ist. Auf diese Weise ist die Klaviatur g völlig vom Klavier trennbar. Dieses Zwischenglied a wird mit Erhöhungen h aus Lederfilz o. dgl. angefertigt.

PATENT-ANSPRUCH:

Klaviatur für Pianos, dadurch gekennzeichnet, daß sie um Zapfen am hinteren Ende drehbar und in beliebig schräger Lage spielbereit feststellbar ist.

Hierzu 1 Blatt Zeichnungen.

Clark's patent for the inclined keyboard

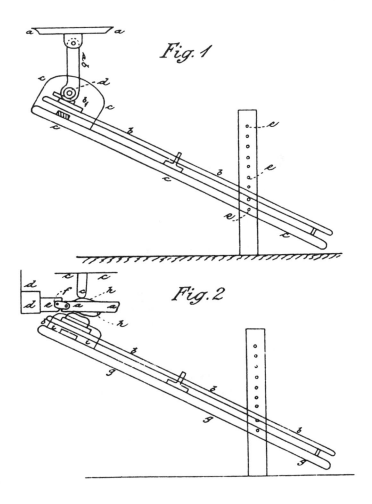

Fig. 1

Fig. 2

Illustration of the inclined keyboard

Clark playing the one-keyboard elevated piano
with an inclined keyboard

Clark playing the final model of his two-keyboard elevated piano with inclined keyboards. The legend (in *Brahms' Noblesse*) states: "Introduction of the Double-Piano by Frederic Horace Clark. Zürich 1913."

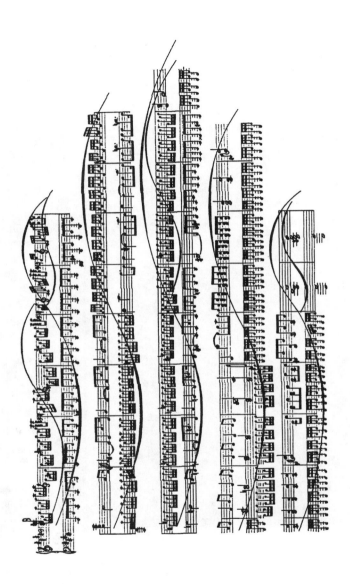

Illustration of rhythmic massings in Beethoven's *Moonlight* Sonata, as found in *Iphigenia*. Probably also a part of *Artists' Unified Editions in Form of Etchings*.

7

The Philosophy of Pure Pianism and Its Consequences

The Philosophy of Pianoforte Music

In 1892 and 1899 Clark published several articles in the journal *Music*.[1] Some of these articles dealt with his philosophy of piano playing, and some were intellectual, or pseudointellectual, analyses of six of Beethoven's piano sonatas.

"The Philosophy of Pianoforte Music" was published in *Music*, the first three chapters in the April 1892 volume, and the remaining two in the May volume of the same year.[2] It is a lengthy five-chapter essay, which Clark often referred to later as a "philosophy of pure pianism." The essay could have been conceived earlier, because it is mentioned in *Iphigenia*, although his wife had died before it was published. This work represents the middle, and probably most valuable, of the three phases of Clark's development. It lies between an early version of his method, spurred by intuition, and the late version, immersed in religion, of his *Pianistenharmonie* (1910).[3]

Writing on pianism, Clark sought to establish a balanced relationship between science on the one hand, and philosophy and intuition on the other. Science was to be represented by the "technological" analysis of the working apparatus and its efficiency in translating the principle of harmony, unity, and universality. The study of those principles and their nature was to be the subject of "morphological" analysis. Both of these were to add up to a complete study of the philosophy of art in general or any artistic discipline in particular. Likening the philosophy of art to the philosophy of nature, Clark points out that the study of nature is prefatory and beneficial to the pure expression of the soul in art. Stating that "everything in nature is found as some mode of motion,"[4] he calls the unity in which this flow occurs an attribute of the eternal harmonic principle, and its manifestations a natural law. As a model of the manifestation of this universal principle of unity, Clark describes a composite sound wave.

Drawing diagrams of four sounds at octave intervals, and showing the resulting wave form as a listener would perceive it, he calls the final composite drawing an "envelopment," and describes it as a "three-fold involuted undulation." Clark compares the harmonious relationship of the curves with the relationship of musical or poetic units toward the whole work.[5]

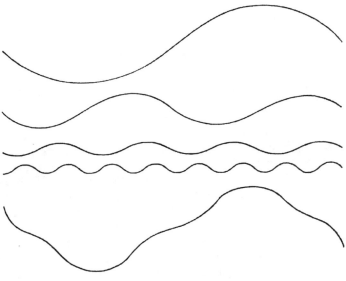

Fig. 7.1. An "envelopment"

In his article Clark maintains that although in poetry one can find metrical and rhythmical forms that are independent of the expressed ideas, in music the form and the contents are unified. Taking an eight-measure period as the most ordinary or smallest unit of form, Clark subdivides it into two halves of four, each of which contains two two-measure groups. These two-measure groups are defined by their principal and subordinate parts, which he calls "stress and lull." He obviously describes here arsis and thesis. Clark transfers their order back to larger groups, thus creating "rhythm-form," a complex series of accented and unaccented units that combine in a unifying, "enveloping" undulation. Here Clark delves into speculation, calling upon "the science of the imagination" to reveal the structure of these abstract formations to the artist's mind. Although at this time he was still inclined toward more rational explanations, Clark does not reject here the role of intuition, either in an artistic creation or in its re-creation. He writes: "The compound nature of musical form may not be produced by means of absolute calculation."[6] Even as the study of unity in nature should be the artist's means of grasping the truth, this very unity has to be created and does not result from randomly grouped mental concepts. The appreciation of the unity of organismal forms created in nature should guide and instruct artists when they are searching for a pure and unified expression in art.

Assuming that a given content can be reproduced best by following the same formal structure that underlies it, Clark asserts that in music, which is a naturally constituted effect, the playing mechanism should accordingly employ curvilinear motions describing cycloids. Curved motions, in a continuous and harmoniously arranged pattern according to variation in volume, thus constitute musically formed tone effects. A complex system of moving masses, such as the pianist's body, could not conceivably function toward the same means unless all of its motions were organized according to the same principle. This organizing form would again be the curve, or its compound variation. In an ideal body, organized according to these principles, the manifestation of force would appear as a curving motion, emanating from a center in motion also created by a higher order of force. Such chains, blended in a continuous "symphony" of dynamic influences, are in turn regulated by the given points of contact with the keyboard. The keyboard does not actually allow an ideal fulfillment of the curvilinear motion, since its resistance feeds back into the playing mechanism and causes deviations in the expenditure of power. The preservation of the interrelations between the moving parts is crucial for the continuation of sympathetic activity. It would therefore also be impossible for any member to remain at rest.[7] An arbitrary or detached motion results from a misinterpretation of the natural action of the human organism[8] and, as such, promotes partial knowledge and a nonunified vision. Taking the natural "eternal principle" and grasping it with an intuition that presupposes the soul's full unity, one creates a transcendental or ideal natural expression.

Subjective Recreation

Clark's analyses of Beethoven's sonatas are based on his understanding of the relationship between form—analytical and physical—and contents, and on his fertile imagination, which here continued to exhibit his increasing monomaniacal tendencies. The sonatas analyzed were those in C-sharp minor, Op. 27, No. 1; in E-flat major, Op. 27, No. 2; in D major, Op. 28; in D minor, Op. 31, No. 2; in F major, Op. 54; and in E-flat major, Op. 81a.[9] In his analysis he tried to recreate the original world of ideas underlying the work. Regardless of how personal the result was, he always tried to heighten the performer's willpower, an understanding of the logical cohesion in a work's inner structure, and imagination in its construction.

The value of these essays lies mainly in the fact that they represent a firsthand report on the evolution Clark's approach to music went through between 1892 and 1899. These years frame the second half of Clark's last period in the United States. Outwardly, the analyses of four sonatas from 1892 are much longer than the latter ones. Also, the copyright footnote does not appear in the 1899 essays. The common feature is the fact that the groups of sonatas appearing in the same year, and consecutive months, are preceded by almost disproportionately long introductions. Thus, in the 1892 essays there is an introduction for sonatas Op. 27, Nos. 1 and 2, but not for Opp. 31 and 54, which appeared a month later. Correspondingly, in the 1899 essays there is an introduction to the Op. 28 analysis, but not to Op. 81a, which appeared in the following month. Whereas the 1892 introduction focuses on differences between the terms and forms of "sonata" and "fantasia," the 1899 introduction is a discourse on the relationship of life and music, and the validity and purpose of adding characterizing titles to musical works. Also, the first group of essays is illustrated with many musical examples, while the second group does not contain a single one.

In the first set of essays Clark writes mostly as a scholar, discussing the form of the sonatas, their place and role in Beethoven's output and, accordingly, the pertinent sentiments relating to the time of creation of these works in Beethoven's life. Clark quite successfully tries to connect details from Beethoven's life and character traits to formal and tonal inflections in the music itself. As one would expect, the "Moonlight Sonata" provides Clark with a reason for a deeper excursion into the realm of religious and philosophic pondering. The following quotation already shows the development of a style which will be typical for Clark after 1900: "The idea of God—the reality of the all-pervading, all-constituting good—is not lost; but it is developed and more definitely recognized, for the individual is aroused to a sense of the infinity from which the freedom or purity of his own individuality depends."[10] It seems that Clark began to write in this deeply reflexive style after his wife's death. The description of sonatas Op. 31, No. 2 and Op. 54 are subtitled "The soul's evolution from ignorance and rebellion to wisdom and blessedness." In the description of the sonata in D minor, "The Tempest," which he calls "The Storm," Clark lets his imagination fly with abandon, but he warns the reader that it is only one of the possible interpretations. He presents a synopsis that deals with the development from a soul's pain, caused by a loss, to a clear vision of the freedom of harmony and the strength that this vision brings. This subject becomes Clark's favorite vision and could quite possibly have autobiographical elements.

The 1899 set of essays oscillates far more often between rational and speculative explanations. The style is more succinct, but the visions evoked are more far-fetched and more difficult to follow: "The cross-grained knot cannot be cut or removed, in shadow or in sunshine, in major or in minor relations, even in defiance and courage, aye, there most, the soul must suffer, its life must be incomplete while its loved one is remote."[11] Clark speaks here of the "Universal Soul of Nature," "Divine Forces," and the "Sabbath of the Soul."[12] These terms show clearly his growing inclination towards metaphysical explanations.

These writings help clarify the transition in style and focus that Clark experienced, and prove that the change, although naturally set up by Clark's character and his life experiences, happened during the last several years he spent in the United States. It seems that the reason for Clark's "extremist" views and ideas was the fact that he, being as conscientious as he was, immersed himself in his speculative philosophy so deeply that he started to lose touch with reality.

Clark used his pseudo-programmatic subtitles even for his recital programs. In *Music* we find the announcement for a series of six concerts that were played in Santa Clara's Academy, near Dubuque, Iowa, and also at the Northern Indiana Normal School, at Valparaiso, Indiana, and the Stevan School, Chicago, Illinois.[13] The first part of those recitals was dedicated to Beethoven's works, and each of them bears an added subtitle, such as "Rebellion against the harmony of unity and because of pain and loss," "Religious contemplation of and ecstasy in the harmonic power," and "Applying the newly found power to life," for the three movements of the Sonata Op. 31, No. 2. Sonata Op. 13 *(Pathétique)* was embellished with the subtitles of "A life bravely battling with inherent limitations," "A hopeful meditation therein," and "Meeting the same with Christian resignation and power." W. S. B. Mathews comments, in the same announcement:

> It will be noted that Mr. Clarke has affixed to each Beethoven sonata a theory to account for its being. These explanations are curious and interesting, although they have no authority beyond that of representing the reflection of Beethoven's music as it touches the consciousness of Mr. Clarke. In other words, they are valid subjectively, only, and it is by no means likely that Beethoven would remember meaning any of these things, saving probably the bars, notes, signatures, tempi and general mood. Nevertheless the recitals ought to be interesting.[14]

The historical value of these essays is that they are among the first, if not the first, in which analysis is attempted by combining rational knowledge of form, structure, and music history with an intuitive, speculative, and necessarily individual approach. Its rarity is in the fact that these irrational aspects were confined to paper—a procedure which, although it automatically destroys the true spontaneous nature of artists' creativity, at least shows the way one particular artist's mind worked in this respect. Attempts of this kind are very rare in nineteenth-century music literature. Although occasionally his mental images might appear exaggerated, it is also probably true that an artist's mind is never vivid enough. Regardless of the value and appreciation given to Clark's attempt, this seems to be another twentieth-century field of research that Clark opened wide in the last century.

Rhythmic Massing

Clark attempted one more experiment and innovation. He tried to outline in graphs the rhythmic and motivic flow in music, using poetic meters as the model. The only source for this attempt seems to be a publication entitled *The Artists Unified.*[15]

In the preface to the series, Clark sets the goal of the edition as "the promotion of knowledge of the harmonizing features of musical thought, expression, and technique." In the preface to Cramer's etudes, written in January 1895, Clark explains his position and attitude toward other piano schools, mostly using terminology and arguments identical to those of his later works, *Brahms' Noblesse* and *Liszts Offenbarung*. He calls the Clark-Steiniger school a scientific school, based on a compound of free or natural motion, thus rejecting completely separate movements of any part of the playing mechanism. Commenting on Clark's method, Carl Faelten, the director of the New England Conservatory in Boston, where Clark was invited to demonstrate his method *to faculty only*, said: "I cannot see that there are any other physiological organs of pianism than the fingers and what they include from their ends or tips to their roots at the elbow."[16]

Clark also mentions other reactions to his and his wife's school. They range from the judgment that the method is fifty years in advance of the public, through an opinion that it is too scientific for musicians, to a complete lack of understanding. A leading pianist (not named) could not understand what sort of edition this was, having no finger marks. Clark quotes at length a review by Calvin B. Cady, apparently a rare "outsider" who at least attempted to analyze the "rhythmic symbolism" and values of Clark's school.[17]

Describing his publication, Clark states that there are two main series: etudes and pieces. The twenty-four etudes, including those by Czerny, Cramer, and Chopin, were structured so that the beginning ones were in simple eight-measure phrases, advancing into irregular and free ratios. About the same number of pieces began with inventions (probably Bach's) and bagatelles (probably Beethoven's), and ended with Bach's fugues and Beethoven's sonatas.

Clark's student, Sarah E. Noble of New Boston, made the pen and ink drawings for the four units (numbers) of this series as a part of her graduation assignment. Each number cost a dollar, and Clark suggested it should be ordered directly from him, "since the music is not by any means to be classed as a business venture" [indeed!].

The six etudes by Cramer, edited by Clark and published in the etude series, are: (1) Op. 30, No. 9 in G major, (2) Op. 30, No. 2 in E minor, (3) Op. 40, No. 30 in F minor, (4) Op. 30, No. 24 in D minor, (5) Op. 40, No. 2 in C minor, and (6) a thus-far unidentified etude in C minor.[18] The main organizational principle of editing is the so-called rhythmic massing, which Clark discusses in several of his books. Rhythmic massing is organized according to a phrase, and supported by identically organized movements of the playing mechanism. The already mentioned relation of 1 : 2 :: 2 : 4 of the parts of the arm describes also the formal proportion in a regular classical phrase—one theme subdivided into two phrases of four measures each. Brahms (or Clark) explains the execution of this form thus in *Brahms' Noblesse*:

> The upper arms make one round for four bars (period) the pro-nation of forearm is dominant in first and in third bars (phrase beginnings) the supination in second and fourth bars (phrase endings) while the hands cycle in vorticing moderation for each bar or motive. Thus my body has coordinate motion with the organic forms of the music and this blending of mind and body is the light of life, the souls realization, the evolution of immortality.[19]

This is how Clark clarifies the graphic layout of his edition:

> The envelopment of spiral double-curves outlines the essential musical proportionment of larger parts in the verses, and pre-figures the poetic subordination of ordinary metres or bar-units of time and expression to the extraordinary time-units, expres-sion-units and technique-units, or compound Rhythm-Forms, embodying trinitary verses, and free groups of these and of stanzas. Within the group of pages showing the music work, when possible, each page presents one of the cantos or larger parts of the music work. Upon each page the stanzas, within each stanza the verses or trinitary lines, and within each trini-tary line the various parts grouped by combinations of phrases, metres and motives, analyze to the eye, and stamp upon the pictorial consciousness of the reader in units of scientific sym-bolism, the comparative values of disparate simple and com-pound music-parts; promoting clearness of perception and freedom in conception of the Relation which underlies music, and is suggested in the unified unfoldings of Musical Art.[20]

The slurs (curves) drawn by Clark seem to indicate the accumula-tion of rhythmic tension in larger phrases, as well as in their subordi-nate units. In the preface to the Cramer etudes, Clark explains that the curves differ from the ones used in the first part of the publication, which he claims was published in 1891. The new curves thus appear to be simpler and not shaded, and the "trinitary" and dual curves are omitted in nearly all verses where they would be implied because of a symmetrical phrasing. The directional aspect of a musical phrase is strongly emphasized, since the illustration makes clear the distance between the "lowest" and "highest" point in the phrase.

Those moments can be freely compared with the trajectory of a vertically tossed ball, where the virtual cessation of movement at the top of the trajectory corresponds to the stasis of the initial moment of a phrase, accumulating momentum ("speeding up" would probably bring unnecessary inadequate connotations) until the top of the phrase, corresponding to the return of the ball, is reached. Although the phrasing is largely already a part of an individual interpretation, art music of the classical era—and apparently this was the era that Clark restricted himself to—is more subject to the general laws of phrasing. The other important aspect of Clark's edition is the graphic breakup of the piece. The length of a staff coincides with the length of a musical phrase, with similar elements in a vertical lineup. This attempt is important for a student of music in terms of clarification and reconstruction of a form. It not only precedes Artur Schnabel's measure numberings in his edition of Beethoven's sonatas,[21] and, more recently, Stanley Shumway's graphic formal analysis of Bach's two-part inventions,[22] but makes a much stronger, more vivid, and more obvious case than Schnabel's method.

Clark suggested that the initial study of the physical organization of rhythmic proportions be done in a group of six to twelve persons, sitting or standing, but not at an instrument. First the rhythm-form ideas were to be formed in the mind, and then gradually associated with voice and with outlines of a well-known piece of art music (preferably from the classical era). The class would silently organize their motions to the teacher's performance of a musical theme. This principle seems to be a kind of applied Dalcroze method, although the explanation is far too superficial and Clark himself totally rejected the Dalcroze method.

An adapted version of Clark's previously published essay "The Philosophy of Pianoforte Music" (see chapter 3) appears at the end of the preface to the Cramer studies.[23] It was supposed to help music students in their development during the rhythm-form classes.

All of the innovative attempts discussed in this chapter combine towards a better understanding of the pieces' formal structure, musical intentions, and extra-musical associations. Clark obviously realized the importance of conscious comprehension of all aspects of musical creativity and, even more importantly, the processes required for the performers' re-creation. The coordination Clark requested among various analytical approaches to a piece is in concordance with, and a reflection of, his general scheme of centrally organized thought and action. In *Liszts Offenbarung*, probably speaking his own mind through Liszt's person, Clark explains the connection thus:

> The secret of my art-technique lies altogether in the absolute unification of the movements of the various parts of my arm with the form of the rhythmic parts of music. Just as a theme, phrases, and motives represent a threefold combination of rhythmic forms, so does the trinitative complex of composite vibration impulses (one in the shoulder joint, two in elbow joints, and four in wrist joints) actually result in a compound, harmonic, and fluent technique—an absolute reflection of the spirit of *logos*, the word which was at the beginning, and which was the God![24]

This organization reflects again the all-encompassing ultimate cosmological and theological scheme, of which Clark was so fond.

Notes

1. *Music* 1 (Chicago: n.p., 1892): 243-63, 368-93; *Music* 15 (1899): 304-11, 431-37.

2. Chapters 1-3 in *Music* 1 (April 1892): 613-20; chapters 4-5 in *Music* 2 (May 1892): 98-104.

3. (Berlin: n.p., 1910).

4. *Music* 1 (April 1892): 615. This is an echo of Heraclitus' *panta rhei* (everything changes) and foreshadows modern atomic theory.

5. The diagrams are shown as drawn by Clark, in his essay "The Philosophy of Pianoforte Music," *Music* 1 (April 1892): 617.

6. *Music* 2 (May 1892): 102.

7. See the description of Deppe's method in Clark's *Iphigenia*, 40-90.

8. Here Clark shows a very firm and unconditional belief in science as the source and help in recognizing and forming a natural approach towards playing and interpretation.

9. Clark omits the "a" in the opus number.

10. Music 1 (January 1892): 254.

11. Music 15 (January 1899): 432.

12. Music 15 (January 1899): 307.

13. Music 19 (November 1900): 84-85.

14. Music 19 (November 1900): 84-85.

15. The full title of what appears to be a series of editions reads: *The Artists Unified or Poetic Edition of Classical Works of Modern Instrumental Music; By Frederic Horace Clark; Being a Symbolization of the Small and*

Large Rhythms or Parts of the Music and Their Envelopment in Verses Stanzas and Groups of Stanzas; The Symphonies and Sonatas of Mozart, Schubert and Beethoven; The Preludes and Fugues of Bach; The Songs Without Words of Mendelssohn; The Etudes of Chopin (Chicago: Pure Music Society, 1891). Another subtitle, appearing above the introductory page of the series, reads: *A Harmonic Analysis of the Prime Features of the Musical Art-Organism.* The Pure Music Society was instituted through the tuition of Frederic Horace Clark, and its editions were available for sale from pupils and teachers of the Clark-Steiniger school, and at Lyon & Healy's music store in Chicago.

The only volume belonging to the series discovered so far is entitled *A Poetic Edition of Six Cramer Etudes; A Series of Musical Form Etchings, Being Studies (First Group of Second Grade) in the Clark-Steiniger Pianoforte School* (Chicago: Pure Music Society, 1895). The four-year lapse between the copyrights probably indicates that at least some of the above mentioned pieces of music were edited and published during that period. There is no definite proof thus far whether any or all of the pieces of music were actually published. However, in the preface to the whole group, the larger part of which is evidently missing, it is indicated that twenty-four Czerny form-studies, twelve pieces by Bach and Beethoven, and the Sonata in G, Op. 14, by Beethoven were also published as parts of this particular group (first group of second grade, as Clark classified it).

16. In 1885, the New England Conservatory was affiliated with Boston University, which was founded in 1873. The "director" of the University's college of music, as it was called at the time, was actually the dean, and he held the position since the university was founded. His name was Eben Tourjée (1834-91), and he was active as an educator, choral conductor, and organist, although Clark referred to him as a pianist.

17. *Chicago Music Review*, ed. Calvin B. Cady, December 1891, January 1892, as quoted in Clark's preface to *Six Cramer Etudes*. The only major concern Cady had was apparently a fear of disconnected patterns and playing that might form in students' minds because of the strophic graphical display of the pieces. This assumption was refuted by Clark, who stated that nothing of the kind was happening in his students' minds since they were taught to develop composite ideas and action.

18. See Appendix III.

19. Frederic Horace Clark, *Brahms' Noblesse* (Zürich: Pianistenharmo-niepresse, 1914), 277.

20. From the preface to *The Artist's Poetic or Unified Edition* (see note 15).

21. Schnabel numbered the consecutive measures in a phrase with as-cending numbers.

22. As yet unpublished.

23. Chapters 1-3 in *Music* 1 (April 1892): 613-20; chapters 4-5, *Music* 2 (May 1892): 98-104.

8

The Three Impromptus Op. 4: A Compendium of the Clark-Steiniger Piano School

As Clark himself stated in the preface, this set of three impromptus was written in Russia, in August 1884. This must have been the second of the two known visits Clark made to the Quellenhof estate, and on this one he was accompanied by his wife. The owner of the estate, which was situated near Riga, Latvia, was Baroness Emilie von Tiesenhauser-Manteuffel. She seems to have been very interested in the arts. After reading Longfellow's poem *Hiawatha*, she asked Clark to set to music some parts that she particularly admired. However, only the third impromptu is supplied with programmatic indications related to the poem. The pieces were also intended as studies for the Clark-Steiniger pianoforte school. After fifteen years of use in teaching, they were finally published in 1900.[1] Each of the pieces is dedicated to a different patron, namely Miss Mary Green of Jacksonville, Illinois, Miss Meta Horner of Medaryville, Indiana, and Miss Charlotte Siellaf of Bellevue, Idaho. All of them had helped in the publication of this set. The copy of the set in the possession of the Newberry Library is dedicated in handwriting to W. S. B. Mathews, the noted American critic and publisher, and dated 20 August 1900. It is important to note that all of Clark's tempo, dynamic, and character indications are in English.[2]

The first impromptu is in B-flat major. Its 128 measures are very clearly divided into A-B(bc)-A form. The middle part consists of two equally long and basically unrelated sections. The second impromptu, 92 measures long, is in D-flat major. It is more complex formally, but its many contrasting units also form a ternary frame. The outer parts consist of scale-passages alternating with chords, while the middle section is more intimate and melodious. The last impromptu is the longest (179 measures), the most elaborate formally and technically, and the only one with programmatic tendencies. Its sections are titled "Hiawatha's Heart" (20 measures), "Hiawatha's Pride" (12 measures), "Hiawatha's Moccasins" (24 measures), "Hiawatha's Wooing" (24 measures), "Hiawatha's Returning" (35 measures), and the last and most expanded section, also including an untitled codetta, "Hiawatha's Struggle with the Death Spirit" (64 measures).

The graphic layout of the pieces is somewhat unusual, but appears to be in concordance with the principle of rhythmic phrasing, a principle that Clark obviously advocated not only in his analysis (see chapter 7) but in composing as well. The first unusual feature is that the key signature appears only at the beginning of each page (except in cases of key change) and also at the beginning of each distinct section. This can be interpreted as another means of unification, since an interpreter has to keep a clear and conscious picture of each section as a whole, not having any visual reminder. It is quite obvious that the three pieces progress in formal and in technical complexity. The first impromptu is written and laid out in simple eight-measure phrases. The second one, subdivided in five larger sections, is also more irregular, and only the middle (third) section consists of three rounded eight-measure phrases. The third impromptu's six sections are formally highly irregular, and in this piece the graphic layout helps most to convey its structure.

There are two main features in the set, which give it the distinctive signature of Clark's individuality and innovating approach. They are his musical language and his technical approach. The musical qualities of this set are rather dubious. A certain naiveté of compositional approach pervades all three pieces. This is probably largely due to the fact that Clark apparently tried to incorporate many different technical problems in these pieces, and that they were ultimately intended as studies, rather than performance pieces.[3] Although it is beyond doubt that Clark had received instruction in harmony and counterpoint in Leipzig, he was probably self-taught in composition. His musical ideas and their treatment seem often naive and dilettantish and even his tonal scheme occasionally seems rather odd. But this is perhaps an instance where one has to remember Clark's character and his lack of circumstantial approach.

However, from a musicological and analytical point of view it is certainly more important *what* he wanted to express than *how* he did it. His musical works reveal perhaps the same kind of frankness and directness in his behavior that made him unpopular and difficult to understand. He apparently never knew how to express his ideas in more popular terms, and quite possibly he was inflexible enough not to want to do it anyway. Regardless of an occasional apparent lack of sophistication in writing, the originality of his musical ideas and their forthright notation, the very freshness and "innocence" of the approach make these pieces and their composer related in a special way to Anthony Philip Heinrich, author of *The Dawning of Music in Kentucky* (Philadelphia, 1820).[4] Both Heinrich and Clark had been intensely exposed to western European musical culture—in Clark's case including contacts with some of the most significant musicians and teachers such as Liszt and Deppe. It seems that their backgrounds did not hinder them in finding a unique way to express their highly individual musical ideas in a language that was essentially only marginally related to western musical and pianistic tradition. Heinrich wrote his music solely to express his own feelings, unencumbered by any demand for idiomatic practicality. What ultimately links Clark and Heinrich together is their idealistic visionary approach, and the fact that both of them looked ahead of their times. While Heinrich plunged headlong into romantic style, Clark had a vision of a perfect piano technique of the future. Nevertheless, in writing a piece which was to serve as a study, even though he was trying to advance a new way of thinking about it and mastering it, Clark had to take into account the requirements of standard piano repertory. A study, no matter how individual, has to cover certain technical formulas. It is probably the lack of rapport between his uncompromising spirit, temporarily forced to yield, and the requirements of standard repertory, that makes the first two impromptus less convincing and fortunate.

The last impromptu certainly stands out as having compositionally, artistically, technically, and historically the greatest weight.[5] It must be mentioned that this musical painting of select scenes from Longfellow's epic appeared nine years before Dvořák's ninth symphony, "From the New World", and that it is probably the first musical illustration of "Hiawatha." There is a mixture of almost untraceable stylistic elements in his writing. Naive as they may seem, they also appear very pure and free of excessive influences, which, as mentioned, one might expect from Clark's background. The modal elements in this piece, including the interval of the augmented second, suggest some Slavic influence. This is probably due to the fact that Clark composed these pieces in Russia. The harmonic progressions are late romantic and often involve enharmonic changes. The freshness of the ideas and their treatment leave an incomparably deeper impression than in the first two pieces.

The glimpse of the more valuable traits of Clark's personality as a composer, which shows in this piece, makes one wonder if his self-imposed western education has not actually spoiled Clark's original ideas. The first two impromptus, although definitely more superficial, bear the simplicity and directness of Stephen Foster's melodic ideas. It might be that, since Clark was never educated as a composer, Europe left only a partial imprint on him. Compared to John Knowles Paine, who represents a case of complete conversion of American spirit to the western European musical idiom, Clark seems to have been left with one foot in his home country, and one foot in the Old World, lacking the ultimate conviction to finish the move either way because of his incomplete education.

As far as technical requirements, the first impromptu requires good legato and dexterity in scale patterns of broken double thirds, all in a moderate tempo. The second impromptu is already much more demanding. Its problems consist of fast and powerful diatonic and chromatic scale playing, both in parallel and contrary motion, parallel triadic arpeggios spanning four octaves, and, in the middle part, voicing and legato playing. Technical demands in the third impromptu make it almost transcendental, with technique that combines typical textures of Liszt and Balakirev. Fast scales in one hand, in both hands, and in thirds, abound. *Martelatto* octaves, trills in jumps, and chords in jumps contribute to make this piece a compendium of romantic piano technique.

It would be very difficult to judge the practical aspects of the Clark-Steiniger piano method only by Clark's writings. Fortunately, very detailed fingering indications in the three impromptus offer an excellent insight into specific requirements of the method. Fingerings are present almost without exception for all passages consisting of faster note values. By observing the fingering patterns and their relationship to topography, it is possible to determine and analyze the required movements of the playing apparatus. There is one particular pattern that provides a clue to the practical application of Clark's "double-curve inverted eight" idea. It is found already in the fifth measure of the first impromptu and also in all similar topographical constellations. It is not customary, according to standard piano technique, to start a descending scale pattern in the right hand with a thumb, especially if the hand is approaching it from the left. However, Clark insists on such fingering even in cases where the descending pattern starts on a black key (Impromptu 1, measure 13). This fingering indicates two facts: first, that it takes a special curvilinear approach to the pattern to execute such fingering, and, second, that the expected suppleness of the joints involved in the motion is quite above the average.[6]

Fig. 8.1. Impromptu 1, measures 5-8 and 13-16

Negotiating the transition from the fourth to the fifth measure with a standard fingering, and starting the descending figure probably with the fourth finger, one would expect a shallow curvilinear motion which would bring the forearm on either a downward or an upward curve to the required position, with the fingers covering already the initial four notes, from *d''* to *a'*. The implication of Clark's fingering is that the forearm has to clear the position completely and approach it from the right side. This can be done only with a very supple and highly coordinated pronation, combined with either fast sinking of the wrist to a point below both the knuckles and the forearm, if the approach is from above, or a quick "flip" of the wrist, if the approach is from below. Thinking in terms of graphic representation of such a movement, it appears that the position just before the execution of the descending pattern is at the far right side of a horizontally placed oval. Continuing through the four descending figures (measures 5 to 7), it becomes obvious that the top of each of those figures is to be reached in an identical physical approach. The connection between the initial position for each figure is possible only by following with the wrist through the rest of the oval circumscription. This results in a chain of ovals with tiny loops between them—a graphic representation absolutely coinciding with Clark's (see illustration). Moreover, by allowing for the movements of the wrist during this sequence, the forearm has to move in advance, freeing the space for the wrist, and thus forming the double curve that Clark emphasized so much. The combination of movements of the wrist and the forearm results then in an inverted eight figure—the basic graphic representation of Clark's method. This combination of movements is literally the same as the one described by Liszt and Brahms (see chapters 5 and 7).

The greatest difficulty of the method and the final proof that Clark fully implemented his method in his teaching is the fact that there is no other way of executing this figure beginning with the thumb on a black key except by circumscribing a sizable ellipsoid with the arm. Since the axis of this movement is at an angle to the length of the keyboard, the movement itself is partially obstructed by the fallboard. This difficulty was later denounced by Ortmann (see chapter 6) and eliminated by Clark's later model of an inclined keyboard. It is also inevitable that this general movement of the whole arm be accompanied by smaller movements of the subordinated levers, in order to execute the smaller groups while keeping the general direction. This relationship can again be organized according to Clark's double-proportion system.

Analyzing the rest of the fingerings, one can easily discern that not only is there not one instance where Clark requires an isolated and angular movement, but also quite often his fingerings prevent a player from attempting such movements. These conclusions prove the integrity of Clark's theory and his practical approach. Whatever his later claims for true sources and implications of this method were, it is a fact that, after thorough analysis of the physiological properties of the playing mechanism, Clark was able to implement them fully, and thus form the first complete scientifically based method of piano playing.

Notes

1. The date of the preface is erroneously given as August 1890, although Clark himself states that the pieces were in use fifteen years before publication.

2. Only in the first impromptu he once uses "Fine," and "Da Capo al fine," but in the last impromptu he replaces it with "End."

3. Clark did occassionally include them in his concert programs: they appear in the above-mentioned advertisement of his six-concert series in Valparaiso, Dubuque, and Chicago in 1900.

4. (Reprint, New York: Da Capo, 1972).

5. See Appendix B.

6. Clark related that Brahms was the first pianist to attract his attention to the significance of starting a motive or a group with the thumb. This he observed in the 1877 concert in Leipzig, discussed on p. 18.

9

Clark and His Contemporaries

During his lifetime Clark was known as an able musician, but somewhat "unworldly," as W. S. B. Mathews put it. The theory he was advancing and the practice he was demonstrating were far too unconventional for the majority, even when they were not qualified to judge them. There was always a "label" attached to his name and person, and gradually his colleagues showed more and more prejudice, refusing to listen to anything he suggested, being convinced that his thinking was "tainted" by religious and philosophical radicalism. This attitude remained prevalent after his death, and thus, during the following eighty years, he was as good as forgotten, and mentioned in but a few specialized works.[1] In order to try and reassess his position, one must return to his era and peruse some written reviews and criticisms of his work. Most of these come as quotations he himself used in his writings, most frequently in his journals *Music of the Future and of the Present* and *Das Musizieren der Zukunft*. One might question the verisimilitude of those quotations, which come from a person who has distorted the historical truth more than once. However, virtually all were printed in these journals, and include the date and the name of the original newspaper, and often the name of the reviewer as well.

A Musician's Review of Reviews
and of Music and of Life

This was the subtitle for Clark's journal *Music of the Future and of the Present* and probably the most suitable title for a section in which Clark's own thoughts on and reactions to other musicians and people he had contact with help to reconstruct his vision of the world—musical and otherwise. It is difficult to appreciate the driving force in him and the frustrations he was exposed to, without feeling through his words the slights that came his way for many years.

Understanding and conveying musical syntax was of utmost importance for Clark. Therefore, he protested against a mechanistic approach to music, such as von Bulow's manner of numbering bars five apart throughout the work, as well as Barth's, in Berlin, according to which his students were supposed to begin or end playing at any casually named bar. He welcomed the example of Prof. Jacob Hahn, the founder of the Detroit Conservatory of Music, who divided the work by musical lines (as Clark advocated). Clark's dislike of impersonal and automatic interpretation is made clear in the following amusing comparison: "There is no more kinship between metronomic procedure and musical rhythm-massing than there is between a mud turtle and the original American Eagle, . . ."[2] However, he always stood up for analytical and rational analysis. When, on one occasion in Berlin, Amy Fay apparently told him that "logic has nothing whatever to do with music"[3] he replied in his article that "there is nothing in real life nor in true art . . . that is not an embodiment of logic." Clark also commented:

> In degree as pianists come to know the different numbers of bars in bar-groups, or phrases, they will grow to play them with proportionately different importance, faster or slower, softer or louder (unless they cling to the fatal metronome) and then when they thus come to express somewhat the proportionate form-members, pure music will be heard and practiced instead of the monotony and uniformity of the present-day so-called music.[4]

The resulting description of musical texture, apart from its poetical coloring, has certainly proven its value in this century, and cannot be labeled as "far-fetched" from the point of view of modern interpretation.

Music is not the manifestation of straight lines nor is rhythm, nor tone, nor any form of life. Every tone in a bar, every bar in a phrase, in music must be as varied as is every sound and syllable and compound word and member of sense in a line of language. Music is an infinitely intricate composition of mobile worths, of vanishing values, the spirit of whose relations is to be caught and comprehended as hardly by the rapt and scanning and schooled soul as are the aerial changes which transmit from the sun-light the faintest flush of color into, or the breath of perfume from the most delicate rose that blooms. . . . And yet all published methods of pianism now known begin, continue and end with the false mannerisms of independent finger exercises![5]

Clark was able to find fault with even the most feted artists of his time. His opinion of Teresa Carreño, for example, was summed up in the following declaration:

Her Beethoven playing . . . is like a magnificent stone pavement. It gives one a similarly indestructible faith that it is a safe place upon which to walk and ride; but soon we see the pavement nor the sense of its security have neither of them aught to do with the manner in which we walk. It is a kind of art which seems external to the soul. (Can an artist's soul become external?)[6]

In 1903 Clark was at Busoni's concert in Beethoven Hall in Berlin, noticing that the pianist was using so much strength from his back muscles that he was in reaction actually jumping up from his seat. This was an unforgivable extreme in Clark's eyes. However, eight years later, Clark heard him again, in his last Liszt recital, and observed a change in Busoni's approach, whereby he was controlling those large movements through his spine.

In December 1905 Clark heard a Prof. Pembauer playing in Gewandhaus in Leipzig. He wrote to him afterward, congratulating him for the manner in which he constructed his tempi in Chopin's Ballades. After an exchange of opinions, Pembauer wrote in *Internationale Musikgeschichtliche Zeitung*:

But the actual goal of all technical discoveries will be reached only when, after Clark's example (see his 1885 work *Die Lehre des einheitlichen Kunstmittels des Pianisten*), we rediscover the ratio between the musical phrases, the proportions of their first and second parts, and the corresponding interaction of upper arm, elbow and hands, and maintain them in teaching.[7]

Clark was very annoyed by superficiality and lack of knowledge of music "professionals," especially critics, mentioning the case of Paderewski, who played a Beethoven concerto in such a monotonous manner, that the critics found an excuse for him, saying that the music was too classical to allow Paderewski to be musical!

On rare occasions, and even rarer without a qualification, Clark was able to issue praise, when something in an intepretation struck a sympathetic chord in his system: "Madame Zeisler stands at the head of the list, as the best artist, because inside of the bars she has a finer feeling of more and less tone for first and last, for "good" and "bad" beats of the bars, she has a more strong realization of the phrase by intuitive rounding out of the same. . . ."[8] Also, he regarded positively the work of William Mason, who, quoting Liszt's words in *Liszts Offenbarung* "learned the method of playing from below upwards, and published it in New York. . . . Mason's touch . . . can not happen without different parts of the body participating, and that is the first step towards future understanding of my [Liszt's] art . . . .[9]

Finally, here is a prediction by Clark, cynical but perspicacious, and not too far off the mark: "In the year 2000 musicians will not be able to achieve a high position before they defend their doctorates in at least seven different areas, and all of that to implement directly science in the practice of playing."[10]

Clark and His Colleagues

Regarding his qualifications of the relationship he had with his colleagues, some of them are confirmed indirectly (such as Breithaupt's recognition of Clark's precedence over Bandmann), and some, in light of all the evidence, simply make sense. One shouldn't forget that, if anything, Clark was seen by a great many of those who knew him as "a man to be loved." Quite a few of his acquaintances also believed that "a more childlike man has rarely lived."[11] Mathews stated that Clark is mentioned in Amy Fay's *Music Study Abroad* [sic] because he was one among the original crowd of Kullak pupils who discovered Deppe and went over to him. In the following month's issue Mathews was obliged to alter this statement, having received a heated denial by Miss Fay, who protested that Mr. Clark is not in her book, that he never studied with Kullak, was not one of the original discoverers of Deppe, and came to ask her for advice about a master, at which point she suggested Deppe and Steiniger to him. Apparently at about that time Clark invited her to the Music Conservatory in Detroit, where he was teaching, and they gave a concert together. He appears to have been utterly disgusted by the "finger-falling tone-production" shown by Fay. Following this incident, Fay wrote to him several times, or at least Clark claimed he still had the letters Fay wrote to him between 1881 and 1885, trying to "seduce" him into Deppe's camp, while he was studying with Ehrlich.[12] Knowing that he had read Ehrlich's book on piano practicing in 1880, which inspired him to his first writing on the subject, one can surmise that it is likely that this was the reason why Clark studied with Ehrlich upon his return to Germany. This also makes Clark's version (see chapter 1), according to which he was simply asked by Fay to deliver a book to Deppe, more plausible. In 1890 Fay wrote an obituary for Deppe in Boston, in which she apparently mocked Clark's "spiral system." In 1901 Clark stated that "no one but Miss Amy Fay comes anywhere near him [Mathews] in writing in such a peculiarly surpassing vein of inconsistency!"[13]

A particularly interesting aspect of Clark's activities is related to their public presentation. He confirms indirectly, through cross-references and quotations in his writings, especially the journals, that he was indeed the first one to come up with certain ideas and their practical application. However, he felt that some of his colleagues have unjustly appropriated his thoughts and tried to integrate them into their own playing and teaching systems. The persons whose names are constantly interspersed throughout Clark's articles are Tony (Antonia) Bandmann, Friedrich Adolf Steinhausen, Ludwig Deppe, and Rudolf Maria Breithaupt, all of who he loathed for being unfair, taking advantage of him and presenting his achievements as their own, and for trying to disseminate playing techniques which for him had very little true foundation.

Thus, Clark claims that Bandmann, while his student, translated into German Clark's theory of "spiral system" in 1899 and showed it to Steinhausen, who in 1903 was already using it as his own term. Some of the "priority"-related issues became quite intricate, as this paragraph, written in the third person, shows:

> In 1905 Steinhausen wrote that Clark's "cycloids" are physiologically wrong, even if physically correct, and that therefore one shouldn't train "art-movements" [*Kunstbewegung*, one of Clark's terms for his coordinated system of movements].[14] In 1907 Bandmann wrote that there shouldn't exist a technique which is a purpose in itself, but expressly does not consider Clark's system to be an example of such a technique. However, in Steinhausen's introduction to Bandmann's *Weight Technique* (1907) the "chief general doctor" says that Bandmann's

"music-image movement"[15] *(Notenbildbewegung)* system is ingenious and totally her own invention. Bandmann, however, studied even before its publication Clark's edition of Beethoven's sonatas, where Clark had this movement illustrated and printed quite clearly in 1890 .... However, even more interesting is the fact that this particular system of movements can not possibly be executed on the piano without the cycloids! According to Steinhausen, that would be physiologically wrong! One can not perform any such music-image without a curvilinear movement, and without an "art-movement" there is no curve, because in the curve lies the art! And, even more obvious: the art and the curve are an end in themselves![16]

Furthermore, Clark affirms it took Bandmann seventeen years to detach herself openly from Deppe's method and then, in 1885, start trusting in Clark's, and a further seventeen, from 1890 to 1907, to appropriate Clark's "rhythmic massing." In retrospect, Steinhausen is seen by many (as, for example, by Karl Wilhelm Engel, in his *F. H. Clarks Liszts Offenbarung als Wegweiser zu einer naturgemäßen Körpermechanik des Klavierspieles*[17]) as the only theoretician except for Clark (as a reflection of Liszt) who continuously expressed the physiologically-based need for an indivisible playing apparatus in *all* playing forms.

A similar situation arose with Anna Steiniger's teaching based on *Eutonie*, which Clark describes as "tension"—today a somewhat unfortunate term, which however at the time implied elasticity.[18] Deppe fought for ten years against this notion, protesting—quite correctly— that it interferes with his notion of "free fall."[19] Caland and Breithaupt, however, followed Steiniger's thinking, for which Deppe never forgave them. In fact, eighteen years later, Caland took Steiniger's idea, exaggerated it as a "fixation" and explained it as a "development" of Deppe's idea. Bertrand Ott, in his *Lisztian Keyboard Energy,*[20] points out that Caland's second book *Die Ausnutzung der Kraftquellen beim Klavierspiel* (The utilization of the sources of energy in piano playing) was a revision, influenced by Clark, of the notions of weight and inertia, as taught by Deppe and published in her first work.

Dr. Walter Niemann wrote an article in *Neue Zeitschrift für Musik* in which he affirmed that Clark's "unifying doctrine" of 1885 served as the basis for Caland's so-called "expansion" of Deppe's teaching and of all similar attempts.[21] In a footnote Clark seems to have started losing his patience:

I have been waiting for quite a while for Miss Caland to admit publicly that her "expansion" of Deppe's idea is but a one-sided and backward application of my teaching. If she decides not to do it, I shall reveal the personal reasons which have led her to misrepresent my teaching and to distort Deppe's.[22]

In another footnote Clark sums up the whole episode:

If Caland is able to prove that Deppe taught breathing exercises (or muscle-tensing or curves or any "round" movement whatsoever), by doing so she would be emphasizing many of the valid points that Deppe took over from me. I have proven in writing to Dr. Heuss in 1905 that I have taught all of these and other basic notions of Deppe-Caland "expansion," in strict opposition to Deppe's teaching, to Caland at the beginning of 1885.[23]

The only real merit Clark saw in Deppe's work was Deppe's continuous effort to eliminate the key-hitting and any type of "attack" on the key.

This is how Clark, again writing in the third person, explains his relationship with Breithaupt, who apparently met Caland through Clark:

Schroeder, Dina van der Hoeven's groom, brought him [Breithaupt] secretly in December and January 1903-04 Clark's writings and manuscripts. At that time said Schroeder in Clark's apartment, before three witnesses and Clark, that because Clark had dared to say that Carreño is not his artistic ideal, Breithaupt wants to destroy Clark and his teaching, is able much more than Clark to write a book on Clark's natural technique, and will dedicate it to Carreño. . . . Dina van der Hoeven and her groom, just as others from Carreño-circles, pressed themselves around Clark in 1903 in Berlin, just as many others did in Boston, New York and Chicago, in Clark's lectures on natural piano technique from 1885-1900. . . . On this subject I received a letter from "la Mara" in 1906, stating that she knows no pianist better than d'Albert and Carreño, and also knows of no person less inclined to think philosophically about technique, since any harmony has to reside on the philosophical basis for the practice. Following this comes even more poignant the last of the repeated statements of d'Albert: he is not an artist as a pianist, but as a composer, as he plays from pure love and talent, and without reference to any method.[24]

Clark as a Musician

One of the first descriptions of Clark's musical aptitude comes from Mathews:

> The scholarship of Mr. Clarke is prodigious, and it is not the theoretical scholarship of the German pedant, but a good right down reliability at the keyboard. . . . he is able to play at call practically the whole of the thirty-two sonatas of Beethoven, with an especial leaning towards those of the last period; pretty much all the great piano works of Schumann, Chopin and many of those of Liszt.
>
> All of this playing is characterized by the intelligence of a man who feels every note and understands exactly whither the tonal web is momentarily tending, its texture of inner voices, its psychological significance and a poetic intention of story attached or semi-attached. In short, there are very few pianists anywhere able to quote at call a larger chapter of the best literature of the piano. I scarcely know precisely where Mr. Clarke falls something short of being a superior performing virtuoso, for virtuoso in some degree he surely is. No man has a purer faith in music; none a surer discrimination between that which means and that which does not. Yet, while it is playing to respect, to admire, it is also to criticize. He is often too loud and his finger work is rather under done. On the other hand, he has great breadth and earnestness. I imagine that his peculiarities of technique are his own, due to a rather superlative reaction against what he calls the German "finger-knocking system," meaning thereby the German method of regarding finger action as the be-all and end-all of the pianist.[25]

Clark's words in December 1901 appear as an indirect, but related, answer:

> You will find that he [Mathews] says my playing is entirely different from that of the pianists of the present day. . . . When I shall have so realized the universal laws of art, as I have discovered them applied to pianism, what the people will see that my pianism is essentially different from that of others, then will my life [for] the last twenty years have proved to have been led by the spirit of good for all mankind. . . . All separate member-movements, such as hand or finger hittings, can only spell words, letter by letter; but I talked of a single motion which could pronounce words, enunciating many letters with one effort![26]

Continuing his article, Clark proved that he didn't care much for Mathews's opinions, even if they were positive:

> Mr. Mathews wrote of my playing in his music magazine in October or September 1900, "No one knows better the value of every detail in the art of music than Mr. Clark." I did not use this commendation in my circulars because I have not deemed that Mr. Mathews knew what he was saying if he could say this of me and yet admire and deem musical such featureless playing as Godowsky's.
>
> Another thing Mr. Mathews always thought of my art was, as he writes "I cannot see wherein Mr. Clark's playing seems to fall short of virtuosity." Of course he cannot see this because his idea of virtuosity in common with that of the present musical world is the idea-less and monotonous stuff of the present times in way of metronomic and finger-hitting monotony which dazzles solely by its celerity. Feats of such a kind are called virtuosity! . . .
>
> I am really satisfied to suffer all I may have to suffer from Mr. Mathews and his public on account of their little-mindedness of admiration for low, mechanical glitter rather than proportionization of detail and comprehensiveness of spirit in musical art![27]

A bit further in the same text, a human confession and an outcry against rhythmical stiffness:

> And why does Mr. Mathews pain me more than the other equally blind "critics," kickers against the classical pricks? Because I love Mathews personally, and because he has written enough about musical form to be responsible to spend tearfully searching days and nights and years to know the relations and values in compound vibrations and rhythms and musical forms and to see that the tone-art is also a time-art and that metre-varieties are the only means creating proportions and harmonies and unities in the time-at. Shame upon the folly of the metronome . . . and its perpetual employ by "great musicians" during their life-time![28]

A. C. Klein, the director of the Dubuque Academy of Music wrote Clark a note on his concert: "Just a few lines to thank you once more for the great pleasure I had yesterday in hearing you play the Chopin Etudes. . . . Your playing was so dignified, so noble and uplifting that I love to recall it, in fact I have been filled with it ever since."[29]

George H. Wilson, musical editor of *Boston Evening Traveler* (secretary of World's Fair Music Bureau), opined:

> Whatever system of pianoforte technique may govern the play-
> ing of Frederic Clark—and the subject is one in which there are
> many investigators—the result is unquestionably a tone of re-
> markable purity. A subordination of the mechanics of the art to
> the control of the mind is apparent in the freedom with which
> he plays everything, while the character which he imparts to
> the Beethoven Sonatas, for instance, is another strong proof
> that with him the will and the deed are true affinities. He shows
> that devotion to his work and an appreciation of its dignity
> which lifts his interpretation into the highest channels.[30]

Another praise, written in December 1893 by W. H. Thorne, editor of the *Globe Quarterly Review* in New York City:

> I am well satisfied that Mr. Clark is the one man the world has
> been waiting for to give us a full and perfect rendering of Bee-
> thoven. His playing of Beethoven is simply the completest, the
> most profound, and the most wonderful thing I ever heard in
> the realm of pianoforte playing. Frederick Clark is to Beetho-
> ven and the piano what Ole Bull was to the violin . . . His touch
> is at once soulful, muscular, unerring, brilliant and masterful.[31]

And at the same time Clark himself wrote that "the art of rendering Beethoven music is not yet in its swaddling clothes. It is scarcely born.(!)"[32]

An unidentified reviewer wrote in *Musikalisches Wochenblatt und Neue Zeitschrift für Musik*, on 7 November 1907: "I myself can not hope to find any advantage in Clark's changes because, if the stronger muscles might be relieved by them, then the weaker ones will be straining more."[33] The same reviewer ends his review with the words: "The implementation of Clark's idea makes piano playing more difficult, rather than easier."[34] Clark agreed completely with this statement, reminding the reader that the most precious works of art indeed do sometimes entail the dedication of one's whole life, and nobody doubts the truth of this fact, unless the subject is musical research. Another review, by Paul Merkel, in *Leipziger neueste Nachrichten* of 2 November 1907, starts with the sentence "If the issue would not at least be so serious."[35] Answering this rhetorical wish, Clark points out that at the beginning of each of his journals the printed motto by Goethe declares: "True art is grasped with deep and unshakable seriousness."[36]

Another review, by Arthur Smolian, shows that there were some individuals who at least tried to evaluate Clark's action without prejudice:

> Like alchemists of the Middle Ages and many discovery-eager later-age dreamers, who sacrificed everything that they had, or even more than they had, to a realization of a wish, an idea, and ended as beggars, so has experimental pianist Frederic Horace Clark, born in America, and physically, physiologically and musically educated, given up all the benefits of an ordinary professional life in order to discover the meaning and the sense of some remaining problematic aspects of piano playing, particularly the esthetical and physiological basis for a artistic and harmonious interaction of psyche and body. . . . Lately Clark tried to advertise his piano method himself, so that yesterday he performed in the hall of the Künstlerhaus standing, in front of a piano raised on high supports, and for an astounded audience, the thirty so-called "Goldberg" variations by J. S. Bach and several works by Liszt . . . the performance has confirmed the plausibility and, necessarily, the purpose of playing only with rotating movements of members. At any rate, one can not deny that there is certain interest for the seriousness of his research, and for his idealistic discoverer-impulse, which has partly resulted in some quite accurate discoveries.[37]

The truthfulness and accuracy of Clark's quotations and references are reinforced by the fact that he quoted without compunction all the negative opinions about himself as well, albeit first and foremost in order to counterattack. Another review of the same concert, by a Dr. Heuss, who was an editor for the *Zeitschrift der internationalen Musikgesellschaft* and reviewer of *Leipziger Volkszeitung*, shows a rare even-handed approach.

> A detailed analysis of Frederic Horace Clark's playing (Künstlerhaus) should be made here, because the matter is more important than all the season's piano evenings put together. . . . Liszt, the greatest of all pianists, has in his mature age never beaten on the piano, and Clark's efforts are made in order to explain and scientifically analyze Liszt's playing. Today's pianists play everything with fingers and forearm, and, Breithaupt's effective book in which he advocated some changes notwithstanding, one has to conclude that Clark has presented those theories in a much purer and complete manner at the time when Breithaupt was but a little boy. All the gentlemen and ladies, who have in the recent years written about

piano playing, such as Steinhausen, Breithaupt, the ladies Caland and Bandmann, founded their work directly or indirectly on Clark's, giving in part a full recognition of Clark's own goals.

It is now quite obvious that Clark's playing does not show any hardness in the least, that he produces a tone which is healthy and full, and thus differs quite significantly in a purely pianistic manner from others. . . . Furthermore, one has to conclude that Clark's playing on the other hand leaves something to be desired, that his trills sound unprepared. We ourselves do not consider him as the ideal representative of his method. . . . If a piano genius like d'Albert would and could (for Clark's method presupposes a complete change), then we would witness a pianistic miracle that has not happened since Liszt. . . . One can hardly avoid mentioning that Clark has performed many a variation with certain dragging, probably due to his own character, and ignored their rejoicing and carefree aspects.
. . .

One more impression should be mentioned here: Clark's system of proportions occasionally is all too obvious, the application of the theory is too open and reveals the organism of the piece too clearly. The listener should not always be reminded of the principles the performer is using . . . I personally know, of the whole army of pianists in Germany, only one who dares to perform the work (Goldberg variations) in public, R. Buchmayer in Dresden. . . . Clark has documented his teaching in various books, lastly in *Liszts Offenbarung* which, being throughout in a philosophical spirit, requires complete attention from the reader and can not be recommended enough to any musician, in particular a pianist. . . . it was quite typical that the local pianists were very sparsely represented at the concert, although nobody can claim that any of the whole army of those factory products of the conservatories possess something that is at least remotely akin to an idea. . . . On December 3 Clark gives his second evening, with the five last Beethoven Sonatas, a program which is unfortunately too long. It will however cause even more controversy than the first concert, which can not prevent us from regarding the core of Clark's method as the truth.[38]

After Clark's concert in Singakademie, Professor Carl Stumpf of Berlin University expressed in writing an opinion that many of his learned colleagues certainly shared: "Your piano playing is neither better nor worse than that of other talented virtuosi; therefore I see no advantage in your method."[39] This was apparently an echo of a well-known phrase by Kullak "Do as you wish, as long as it sounds well."

Clark strongly objected to such an opinion, according to which all methods are pedagogically equally valid, as long as they produce a satisfactory result.

Clark, who in 1911 did not call himself any longer a "pianist" but a "harmonizer," felt that the "harmonizing" activity during a concert amounts to a religious, or at least spiritual activity. Therefore, he included in his 1911 concert program in Jena a note which read: "Since the harmonizer seeks to create the wholeness and the unified nucleus of movement, and since the applause represents a turmoil of separated and broken, i.e., unharmonious activity, may the audience refrain from the applause."[40] In a review of this concert, Dr. Max Fincke wrote:

> The arms in concordance with the periods of the music, performed complete ellipses, while the hands spiralised first inwards, then outwards, now indrawing, then out-pushing in concordance with the motives. The ground forms were thus clearly seen in organized working motion. It was plain that a strong tendency unto form, which is essentially the spirit of the musical content, aimed to express itself as inner unifying soul life upon the keys. Perpetually did the arms plastically stature the work of this musical organizing. Unbrokeness and unifying evolution of tone-working motion is Clark's ideal, unto which he subordinates himself with iron consequence and exemplary self-negation, sacrificing all mere effect. He excludes all peripheral technique, every bit of finger-work, every sort of hammer-action, swinging, falling or throwing of "weight-technique," believing that the noblest element of art-work is embodied in these perfect arm and hand cycles which he teaches as the natural expression of the harmonious element of the soul. He has essayed to establish the truth of his art mathematically, physiologically and philosophically. But indeed the deepest element of all in this new art seems to be the idea, that the pianist thus exercises the beauty of the *Harmonie* unto which all noblest life and culture finally strives.[41]

Notes

1. Works by Roës, Ott and Engel—see chapter 10.
2. *Music of the Future and of the Present* Vol. 1 No. 3 (December 1901): 151.
3. As quoted in *Music of the Future* Vol. 1 No. 3 (December 1901): 201.
4. *Music of the Future* Vol. 1 No. 3 (December 1901): 164.
5. *Music of the Future* Vol. 1 No. 3 (December 1901): 169.

6. *Music of the Future* Vol. 1 No. 3 (December 1901): 153.

7. *Das Musizieren* Vol. 2 No. 1 (August 1912): 370.

8. *Music of the Future* Vol. 1 No. 3 (December 1901): 175.

9. *Liszts Offenbarung*, 187.

10. *Das Musizieren der Zukunft* Vol. 1 No. 4 (March 1908): 272.

11. Words of W. S. B. Mathews in *Music* 5 (September 1900): 481.

12. *Das Musizieren* Vol. 2 No. 1 (August 1912): 374.

13. *Music of the Future* Vol. 1 No. 3 (December 1901): 15 (Preface).

14. In *Die Physiologischen Fehler und die Umgestaltung der Klavier-technik* (Leipzig: Breitkopf & Härtel, 1929), 157, Steinhausen writes:

> There can be no rolling movement without a curvilinear movement. Those indicated by Caland are of another sort, and explicable by fixation, but wrong. Clark's curves are correctly observed, but incorrectly explained from a physiological point of view; the source of the curvilinear movement is not the torsion of all members along the longitudinal axes of individual parts of the skeleton, but the rolling movement from the upper arm and, in particular, forearm. Totally correct is the explanation by Bandmann, in which the curving lines are being formed by the movement of the wrist, describing *natural phrasing* [italics mine].

Of course, Bandmann was an enthusiastic supporter of Steinhausen and helped toward practical implementation of his work.

15. See chapter 7, on "rhythmic massing."

16. *Das Musizieren* Vol. 1 No. 4 (December 1907): 237-8.

17. Karl Wilhelm Engel, "F. H. Clarks *Liszts Offenbarung* als Wegweiser zu einer naturgemäßen Körpermechanik des Klavierspieles (1972)," (F. H. Clark's *Liszts Offenbarung* as a signpost towards a natural body mechanics of piano playing) TMs (photocopy), 85.

18. Described in an article in *Lessmans Zeitung* in the summer of 1885, and in Cobb's biography of Steiniger in 1886.

19. For this notion he was, according to Clark, declared a "charlatan" by Moritz Moszkowski and Liszt, during their conversations with Clark in 1882-84. *Das Musizieren* Vol. 1 No. 4 (November 1908): 311.

20. Bertrand Ott, *Lisztian Keyboard Energy* (Lewiston, N.Y.: Edwin Mellen, 1992), translation by Donald H. Windham of *Liszt et la pédagogie du piano* (Issy-les-Moulineaux: E. A. P., nd).

21. *Das Musizieren* Vol. 1 No. 4 (November 1908): 305.

22. *Das Musizieren* Vol. 1 No. 4 (November 1908): 307.

23. *Das Musizieren* Vol. 1 No. 4 (November 1908): 309.

24. *Das Musizieren* Vol. 1 No. 4 (November 1908): 310. Dina van der Hoeven was apparently Carreño's student. Teresa Carreño (1853-1917) was a famous Venezuelan pianist who studied with Gottschalk, Mathias, and Anton

Rubinstein. Eugène d'Albert (1864-1932), himself married six times, was one of her four husbands.

25. *Music* 5 (September 1900): 481-81.

26. *Music of the Future* Vol. 1 No. 3 (December 1901): 10 (Preface).

27. *Music of the Future* Vol. 1 No. 3 (December 1901): 13 (Preface).

28. *Music of the Future* Vol. 1 No. 3 (December 1901): 156.

29. Letter written on October 28, 1901, as quoted in *Music of the Future* Vol. 1 No. 3 (December 1901): 14 (Preface).

30. As quoted in *Music of the Future* Vol. 1 No. 3 (December 1901): 229.

31. As quoted in *Music of the Future* Vol. 1 No. 3 (December 1901): 233.

32. *Music of the Future* Vol. 1 No. 3 (December 1901): 161.

33. Page 914, as quoted in *Das Musizieren* Vol. 1 No. 4 (December 1907): 230.

34. *Das Musizieren* Vol. 1 No. 4 (December 1907): 232.

35. As quoted in *Das Musizieren* Vol. 1 No. 4 (December 1907): 233.

36. As quoted in *Das Musizieren* Vol. 1 No. 4 (December 1907): 233.

37. *Leipziger Zeitung*, 2 November 1907, as quoted in *Das Musizieren* Vol. 1 No. 4 (December 1907): 241.

38. *Leipziger Volkszeitung*, 7 November 1907 (art supplement), as quoted in *Das Musizieren* Vol. 1 No. 4 (December 1907): 241-44.

39. As quoted in *Das Musizieren* Vol. 1 No. 4 (March 1908): 245.

40. *Das Musizieren* Vol. 2 No. 1 (March 1912): 343.

41. Clark's own translation from German of the review in *Jena-Volskblatt*, Nov. 9, 1911, as quoted in *Brahms' Noblesse*, 439.

10

Today's Perspective

Contemporary references to Clark are few in number and often dismissive, superficial, or selective in character. Following extensive reports of Clark's family and activities by W. S. B. Mathews and Betina Walker there are four biographical entries by Jones, Mathews, Howe, and Pratt, the first two of which appeared already during Clark's and Steiniger's lives. Next, one finds the only major encyclopedia entry, in *Die Musik in Geschichte und Gegenwart*, and an entry in the *Yugoslav Music Encyclopedia.*[1]

The more recent the mention, the more summary "judgment" and dismissal of Clark seems to be. Already Pratt mentions a "series of extravagant essays on piano-playing and piano-music," while Johnen comments that "because of far-fetched imagery and expression Clark was not able to find publisher for his later works, which appeared in his own edition. These works could hardly be called suitable for a professional evaluation." Walter Niemann, in his *Klavierlexikon* describes him as a "modern and phantastic piano-metaphysicist, burdened by philosophy and the occult [?]."[2] Continuing this line of "superior disdain" is Alan Walker, who, in a footnote of his edition of the diary of Carl Lachmund, calls Clark a "bizarre character, prowling around the perimeter of Liszt scholarship."[3] In summarily dismissing Clark's statements ("If the reader accepts the story so far, he will have no difficulty in swallowing what happened next."), he shows a typical lack of patience and benevolence, qualities that are necessary if one is to remove the layers of Clark's hermetic and overcomplicated expression, and do justice to the substance of his thought.

Next, one finds Clark's name in an article in which E. Douglas Bomberger tried to establish a definitive register of Liszt's American students.[4] Clark's own *Liszts Offenbarung* and a book by Bertrand Ott (see below) are mentioned as corroborating evidence, although Clark is not mentioned in any other list or discussion of Liszt's students. Indeed, even if Clark played for Liszt and talked with him, he apparently never appeared in a traditional classroom situation, where he would have certainly be mentioned by some other pianists who left written accounts of their study with Liszt. It is therefore probably incorrect to consider Clark as Liszt's student, given the unusual relationship between them, just as it would be unreasonable to consider all of his statements regarding Liszt (and Brahms, for that matter) literally true and factual.

Clark is also mentioned in Gerd Kaemper's *Techniques Pianistiques*, in which he is justly understood as advocating "a conception of the pianistic gesture as an integrated whole over the study of isolated movements of the fingers and hands."[5]

Several recent authors seem to employ Clark's words in such a manner, literally, or with only a fleeting caveat emptor remark. The first of these is Dutchman Paul Roës, whose *Music, the Mystery and the Reality*[6] is a synthesis of his lifelong research of piano technique and musical aesthetics. After analyzing the music and playing of Beethoven, Chopin, Liszt, and Busoni, Roës, himself Busoni's student, tries to answer the perennial question "What meaning has music?" Furthermore, he attempts to reconstruct the method behind Liszt's playing, which is also, according to him, the foundation of what he calls "the school of Weimar" (as illustrated by the playing of Busoni, d'Albert, and Godowsky). The final step is a series (imaginary?) of three lessons according to "Liszt's method," given in a dialogue form, so familiar from Clark's *Liszts Offenbarung*.[7] The prologue of the book is in the form of a conversation in much the same spirit, bordering on metaphysical and speculative, just as, later in the work, is his interpretation of Liszt's Sonata in B Minor, in which the mixture of formal analysis and subjective reading of emotional context do not differ much from Clark's essays on Beethoven's sonatas. When describing Liszt's playing, Roës quotes quite a few observations made by Clark in *Liszts Offenbarung*, while ignoring other contemporary reports (Amy Fay's, for example). The basic idea of Roës's philosophy is, again, very kindred to Clark's, emphasizing the universal character of art, while the author himself, in the preface, laments not having been endowed with a "command [of a] transcendental style that carries the thought beyond the reality of the material." Roës exclaims:

"Alas, this is given rarely to writers!" although one wonders what good did the transcendental style, and the resulting opaqueness of expression, bring to Clark, who was quite a master of it.

The next work in which Clark's name figures prominently, this time side by side with Auguste Boissier, William Mason, Elisabeth Caland, Amy Fay, Marie Jaëll-Trautmann, Carl Lachmund, and August Stradal—most of whom have left firsthand reports and partial analyses of Liszt's playing—is *Lisztian Keyboard Energy* by Bertrand Ott.[8] This work is not only one of the most useful compilations of descriptions of Liszt's playing and its historical evolution, but it goes a step further and, based on those descriptions, attempts to recreate his technique in detail. Some of Ott's expressions really succeed in conveying ideas found in Clark but, fortunately, with more elegance and transparency: "Conceived with a choreography that adopts respiratory dynamics, technique then gives a profoundly human relief to instrumental performances."[9] Ott also quotes some phrases from Liszt's letters, which, although using terminology that Clark would disapprove of as blasphemy, represent most concise summaries of Clark's concept of piano: "The piano, to borrow the original expression of a writer of antiquity, is therefore both microcosm and microdivinity, a miniature world and a miniature god."[10] "All beautiful music must first and always satisfy the absolute, inviolable, and irrevocable conditions of music: proportion, order, harmony and eurhythmy are as indispensable as imagination, fantasy, melody, feeling, or passion."[11]

Considering Clark difficult to fathom, but in essence reliable, Ott recognizes that Clark is a marginal figure for some scholars, and that the poor reception of Clark's ideas in general, and of *Liszts Offenbarung* in particular, was due to a "hazy style, written in poor German by an American who had not mastered the language well."[12] Ott's interpretation of Clark's descriptions of Liszt's playing stresses the impulse of pulling as the force that ultimately determines the adherence of the hand to the keys. This idea would justify Clark's inclined keyboard and the concave keys, both of which facilitate adherence and prehensile action. Finally, Ott recognizes Clark's "synthesizing theory," as he calls it, as being confirmed in general terms by observations made by other disciples of Liszt, as well as by the florid and suggestive "images" that Liszt (or Clark) used to help convey ideas. One specific criticism of Clark's observation is the action of a slightly raised wrist which, in later phases of Liszt's playing, undulated in conjunction with the pulling energy of the arm, and which, according to Ott, was misinterpreted by Clark as an elimination of the angle between the hand and the arm. However, he judges correct Clark's remark that the carpal joint does not act as an independent hinge.

The third and last substantial work in which Clark's words are used extensively is the above-mentioned *F. H. Clarks* Liszts Offen-barung *als Wegweiser zu einer naturgemäßen Körpermechanik des Klavierspieles* by Karl Wilhelm Engel. On 138 typed pages the author starts with Liszt's technical development, his establishment of a coordinated action of all body members and then uses those as the basis for the elucidation of a technical method developed by Paul Pichier (1873-1955), a Viennese piano teacher, who, according to Engel, in the 1940s "reinvented" perfect legato-playing, as developed originally by Liszt and explained by Clark. Engel's knowledge of Clark comes from a rare copy of *Liszts Offenbarung*, which he came across, and from Niemann's *Klavierlexikon*. It is no wonder that he makes some mistakes even in his biographical presentation, claiming, for example, that Clark died in Berlin. However, Engel notices the implausible maturity of the conversations Clark supposedly had as a child with his "grandfather" (actually, granduncle) and that he is not mentioned in any of the larger biographies of Liszt (at the time of his writing). Given that Engel regards as "not without foundation" Deppe's judgment of Clark (which Clark himself quotes in *Liszts Offenbarung*), according to which Clark was no artist, just an enthusiast and a dreamer, it is interesting to note the amount of seriousness with which Engel chose to accept and analyze Clark's words on Liszt's technique.

At the time of his death, Pichier left a large amount of handwritten material dealing with piano technique. That material was arranged by two long-time students of Pichier, Elsa Hesse and Waltraut Ostborne-Paulin, who, with the help of Dr. Walter Krause of the University of Vienna, published a work entitled *Der pianistische Anschlag, Methode und Theorie des Prof. Paul Pichier*.[13] Since Engel saw this work as untrue, with regard to his interpretation of Pichier's thinking, and since Pichier's own style seems to have been itself quite dense, Engel wrote his work as a correction of the other work, and also to facilitate comprehension of Pichier's ideas (a comparison with Matthay and his followers seems unavoidable).

Regarding the position at the piano, Engel finds that Steinhausen's statement, according to which the contact points with the bench are the bases of the mechanical system, is only relatively true, for it is (and should be) the floor on which the feet (as the final members of the body) rest (and where the opposition to the force of gravity begins— my remark). Speculating that this might be the main reason for Clark's playing in a standing position (avoiding one-sided and isolated use of a member), Engel criticizes him for misunderstanding the prerequisites for a free-moving body. Engel sees them in a particular muscular condition that can be described as "standing while sitting" or "sitting while standing." This description is evocative of the Alexander Technique recommendation of an inclined bench, which necessitates firm contact of feet with the floor, alerting the reflexes to an upright balanced position (perhaps related to what Pichier called "amuscular standing"). Pichier's method evidently evolved over a period of years, so that, according to Engel, even some of his oldest students were overrun by the changes in his attitude (would not an imaginary student of Liszt, accompanying him for a period of fifty or more years, encounter the same problem?).

Notes

1. F. P. Jones, *A Handbook of American Music and Musicians* (Canaseraga, N.Y.: F. O. Jones, 1886); reprinted by Da Capo Press, New York, 1971, s.v. Steiniger-Clark, Anna.

A Hundred Years of Music in America, W. S. B. Mathews, ed. (Chicago: G. L. Howe, 1889), s.v. Clark, Anna Steiniger.

Mark Anthony DeWolfe Howe, *Boston Symphony Orchestra 1881-1931* (Boston/New York: Houghton Mifflin, 1931), 259.

The New Encyclopedia of Music and Musicians, Waldo Selden Pratt, ed. (New York: Macmillan, 1939).

Musik in Geschichte und Gegenwart s.v. Clark, Frederic Horace, by Kurt Johnen.

Muzička enciklopedija (Zagreb. JAZU, 1971-77), s.v. Clark, Frederic Horace.

2. As quoted in Karl Wilhelm Engel's "F. H. Clarks *Liszts Offenbarung* als Wegweiser zu einer naturgemäßen Körpermechanik des Klavierspieles (1972)," (F. H. Clark's *Liszts Offenbarung* as a signpost towards a natural body mechanics of piano playing) TMs (photocopy), 5.

3. Living with Liszt: From the Diary of Carl Lachmund, an American Pupil of Liszt, 1882-1884, ed. Alan Walker (Stuyvesant, N.Y.: Pendragon, 1995), 254.

4. E. Douglas Bomberger, "Toward a Definitive Register of Liszt's American Students," *Journal of the American Liszt Society* 33 (January-June 1993): 50-58.

5. Gerd Kaemper, *Techniques Pianistiques* (Paris: Leduc, 1968), 193, as quoted in *Lisztian Keyboard Energy*, 44.

6. Paul Roës, *Music, the Mystery and the Reality* (Chevy Chase, Md.: E&M, 1978), authorized translation by Edna Dean McGray of *La Musique Mystère et Réalité* (Paris: Henry Lemoine, 1955).

7. And, indeed, used already in the earliest teaching manuals (such as Girolamo Diruta's *Il Transilvano*), as an imitation of the Catechism and old Greek philosophical works.

8. Bertrand Ott, *Lisztian Keyboard Energy* (Lewiston, N.Y.: Edwin Mellen, 1992), translation by Donald H. Windham of *Liszt et la pédagogie du piano* (Issy-les-Moulineaux: E. A. P., n.d.).

9. *Lisztian Keyboard Energy*, xvii.

10. Letter by Liszt to Adolphe Pictet, published in *La Gazette Musicale* (February 11, 1838), as quoted in *Lisztian Keyboard Energy*, 1.

11. Letter to Madame d'Agoult (November 15, 1864), as quoted in *Lisztian Keyboard Energy*, 10.

12. *Lisztian Keyboard Energy*, 45.

13. Elsa Hesse and Waltraut Ostborne-Paulin, *Der pianistische Anschlag, Methode und Theorie des Prof. Paul Pichier* (Pianistic touch, method and theory of prof. Paul Pichier) (Graz: Leykam, 1962).

11

Conclusion

The musical world has paid little attention to Frederic Horace Clark. Perhaps he shares the fate of all extreme radicals, regardless of their field. Human society tends to reject out-of-mainstream ideas, especially if they infringe upon the established, legitimized, and profit-making establishments. By the early 1880s Germany already had a net of eleven music conservatories. Those were career- and profit-making institutions, the fame and name of which has also formed the essence of other countries' musical lives (the United States, for example). Musicians graduating from such institutions perpetrated their teachers' attitudes. Their conservative, academic approach was often euphemistically dubbed "orthodox." Any deviation was considered offensive and a threat to the individual's credibility, naturally with consequences for that person's choice of students and remuneration.

This was the situation with which Clark was confronted in Germany. His intricate religious and macrocosmic philosophy and its practical manifestations thus made an all too welcome excuse for all mainstream practicing musicians to reject Clark as a charlatan, epigone, and fanatic. One could think of Janko, Moór, and other keyboard inventors, whose practical but unusual keyboards were ignored for reasons of conservative tradition. It is unfortunate, but typical of historic processes, that even Clark's indisputably innovative and progressive contributions were dismissed together with the questionable ones. One of the reasons was, as one can observe in cases of Caland and Steinhausen, the fact that borrowing ideas and materials was not uncommon at the time, and that authors with stronger mainstream connections were able to push their own or "borrowed" ideas with much more success. The other reason was the obvious ambiguity of Clark's character. His friends knew him to be honest, simple, and straightforward. Although by all accounts he was a loving husband and a caring father, there is no explanation as to the destiny of his family after his final return to Germany. Knowing he had a hard time providing even for himself, it is difficult to imagine him caring for seven other persons at that trying time. His character was formed and drew its strength mostly from his deep religious convictions. Staying true to his ideals was his first law. The uncompromising spirit and persistence with which he enforced this law upon himself and others bordered on singlemindedness. The instances in which he displayed publicly his innermost feelings about some performances were the ones that made him unpopular and a partial outcast. Although he accepted his difficult and unprosperous life as an act of God and fate, he felt bitterness toward those who were better paid for services he thought were not so important for mankind. This bitterness manifested itself also toward fellow musicians who had success and were rewarded for (according to Clark) superficial and irreverent music making, aimed at effect and individual gain.

His direct and unfaltering criticism of all nineteenth-century piano methods, with the partial exception of Liszt's teaching, reveals the fact that in music his beliefs and convictions transcended the laws of social etiquette and were a part of the almost "messianic" drive for a different approach to playing. His position as a musical outcast and "outlaw" reflects the fact that his theory appeared to be out of reach and beyond the grasp of the average trendsetting musician, while his practice seemed unorthodox to the point of ridicule. The apparently narrow and highly functionalistic scope of Clark's perspective was a hindrance to his proclaimed universality of task and purpose.

The seclusiveness of Clark's theory and its author makes a modern interpretation difficult. In the frequent instances where recounting and unfolding of ideas is connected to a well-known personality, it is often perplexing and sometimes next to impossible to find out the necessary historic background and verify Clark's claims. Occasionally, one gets an impression that the described events belong to a tightly written "parallel history" work of science fiction: so vivid and precise are the described events even when common sense would prompt a musicologist to reject a claim made by Clark. Such elusive events are Clark's conversation with Johannes Brahms, as well as the extent of his contact with Franz Liszt. Although both are historically possible, there is no corroboration in any of Brahms's letters, and only a minor one by Liszt. Clark mentions that he promised to Brahms not to reveal anything about Brahms's work on the doctrine of the two-keyboard piano at least during Brahms's lifetime. Whether that is the truth or a cover-up remains to be determined. As for Clark's description of Liszt's person and his playing, it is possible that Clark constructed the story following the already published reports on Liszt and by visiting the historic places. It is more likely, though, especially after analysis of Bertrand Ott's detailed description of Liszt's technique as explained by Clark, and compared to other sources, that Clark makes a valuable historic witness. He explains Liszt's advanced, late-period technique, the refinement and economy of which was basically not fully described, or even less explained, by any of Liszt's late students or followers. After all, Clark never claimed to be Liszt's student, spending apparently only limited periods of time at the summer classes in Weimar. It is more in a role of an artistic "confidante" that Clark sees himself: a role that, if true, would certainly make him a very special person for Liszt and for posterity. For it is well known how reluctant Liszt was to share his innermost thoughts on artistic ideals and piano technique. This premise would also lead to the conclusion that Clark really possessed some of those charismatic, transcendental qualities that were occasionally ascribed to him since his childhood: qualities that would certainly endear him to Liszt.

Furthermore, there is no reason to doubt the sincerity of many pages describing musical life and persons both in Europe and the United States. Scattered among other information, there is a plethora of interesting and sometimes amusing insights on Ludwig Deppe, for example: an important man, the descriptions of whose person, character, and work are almost nonexistent in other contemporary sources. Regardless of the historic exactness in his works and even in his recounting of his own life, one has to regard each word he wrote as a reflection of his ideology and goals. Even if all the facts are not true, they certainly reflect and convey the spiritual and ideological message he wanted to communicate, for his single-minded person and his single-purposed mind were always obsessed with the urge and necessity to transfer his universal ideal to humanity.

At least three elements combine in Clark's philosophy. A Renaissance attitude, with old classical Hellenistic ideals and philosophy revived and reapplied, combine with highly religious hierarchy in which human action mirrors divine actions (thus directly opposing Renaissance human-centeredness), and an incredibly progressive macrocosmic unification, or universality of human purpose. The merging of neoplatonism and Christianity reminds us of St. Augustine. The idea of the divine being mirrored and identified in the human evokes Spinoza's pantheism. The call for unification of mind and matter and of the individual and the universal echoes the creed of Romantic philosophers Schelling and Novalis. This mixture of past, present, and future operates with universal values and combines tightly into a new ethic and esthetic principle. Perhaps his contemporaries in Germany were right to call him a lunatic and a charlatan; perhaps his American contemporaries were right to honor him as the latest and most progressive transcendentalist: in any case, Frederic Horace Clark stands in a quite isolated, but worthy, niche in the history of music and humanity. In purely pianistic terms, the degree of coordination of the mind and the body that he accomplished and demonstrated in the vast repertory he commanded, even if considered superfluous and overcomplicated, makes him one of the most coordinated (physically and mentally) human beings western history knows of, something the East has always tried to achieve. He joins those individuals who never receive the attention they deserve and whose efforts in fighting prejudice, conservatism, and dogmatic approaches, often make them the true representatives of the human spirit, indefatigable in a quest of knowledge and perfection.

Appendix A

F. H. Clark's Concert Programs

These programs appear under the title "Eight Grand Concerts of Pianoforte Music by Frederic Horace Clark in Colleges and Academies," as printed after p. 228 in *Music of the Future and of the Present* Vol. 1 no. 3 (December 1901). The concerts are announced as taking place in September, October, November, and December 1901 and February, March, April, and May of 1902, in Dubuque, Iowa, and Madison, Wisconsin, and also in Indiana, Missouri, and Kentucky, and in Steinway Hall, Chicago. As a matter of curiosity, all programs are quoted exactly as printed, except for obvious typographical mistakes.

I
First Beethoven Concert

Grand Sonata in E flat op. 7
Sonata in D op. 10 No. 3

Andante Favori in F
Bagatelle in D; Bagatelle in C
Grand Polonaise in C op. 89

Appassionato Sonata. F minor op. 57
Twenty-fourth Sonata F sharp op. 78
Grand Sonata in A flat op. 110

II
First Chopin Concert

First Nocturne in B flat op. 9
F sharp Nocturne op. 15 No. 2
First two Impromptus
I. A flat op. 29; II. F sharp op. 36
First two Polonaises, op. 26
I. C sharp minor; II. E flat minor
First two Scherzos
I. B minor op. 20 II; B flat minor op. 31

––––––––

Three Waltzes in minor keys
I. A minor op. 34; II. C sharp minor op. 64; III. E minor
The first Twelve Etudes op. 10
Prelude; Spring rain; Summer night; Passions storm; Fairy dance;
Night; Butterflies; Eroica; Daemon; Soaring; Harp melody; Revolu-
tion

––––––––

The first two Ballades
in F major; in G minor
Grand Concerto Polonaise, op. 22
E flat with Andante Spiriato

III
First Schumann Concert

Papillons op. 2. Twelve impressions of carnival night
Toccata op. 7 in C major

––––––––

Carneval op. 9. 22 scenes Mignonnes

Eight Fantasie Pieces op. 12
Twelve Symphonic Studies op. 13

IV
Bach Concert

Preambule in G
Gavotte in B minor (arranged by St. Saëns)
Fantasie in C minor
Italian Concerto in F

Sixth French Suite

Four Celebrated Preludes and Fugues
Prelude and Fugue in F No. XI
Prelude and Fugue in F sharp minor No. XIV
Prelude and Fugue in G No. XV
Grand Fantasie and Fugue in G minor (arranged by Liszt)

V
Second Beethoven Concert

First Sonata, op. 2 No. 1
Grand Sonata in C, op. 2 no. 3

Grand Sonata in E flat op. 31 no. 3
Fifteen Variations and Fugue upon a theme in the Heroic Symphony

Grand Sonata in A, op. 101
Last Sonata op. 111

VI
Second Chopin Concert

The last two Nocturnes op. 62. B major; E major
Nocturne in C minor op. 48
The last two impromptus
in G flat, op. 51; in C sharp minor, op. 66
Grand Polonaise with mazurka op. 44
Grand Fantasia in F minor op. 49

––––––––

The Last two Scherzos. C sharp minor; E major
The last two Ballades. A flat; F minor
The Second Sonata. B flat minor op. 35

––––––––

Berceuse D flat, op. 57
Grand Polonaise in A flat op. 53
The celebrated A flat waltzes op. 34-42
The last twelve Studies op. 25
Aolian harp; Humming bird; Dancing dimples; Impatience; Hell and
heaven; Venetian night; Meditation; Gayety; Coquette; Battling and
Blessedness; Winter wind; Ocean study

VII
Second Schumann Concert

Kreisleriana op. 16. Eight Fantasias dedicated to Chopin
Grand Fantasia in C op. 17. Dedicated to Liszt

––––––––

Five Novellettes from op. 21
I in F; II in D; III in D; IV in A; V in E
Grand Sonata in G minor op. 22

––––––––

Nocturne in F op. 23
Vienna Carnival first part op. 26
Traumerien in F
Romanza in F sharp major op. 28

Bird as Prophet op. 82
Novellette in B minor op. 99

VIII
Liszt Concert

Twelve Transcendental Pieces op. 1. Dedicated to Czerny

————

II. Grand Polonaise
Concert study of the Ocean
Grand Valse di Bravura in B flat

————

EIGHT TRANSCRIPTIONS
Fantasie on Mozart's "Don Juan"
Schubert's Hark! Hark the Lark
Schubert's Erl King
Mendelssohn's Wedding March
Donizetti's "Lucia de Lammermoor"
Wagner's Spinning Song
Wagner's Tannhauser March
Verdi's "Rigoletto"

Appendix B

F. H. Clark's Impromptu Op. 4 No. 3 "Hiawatha"

This is the last of the set of three impromptus written in Russia, in August 1884. According to Clark, after reading Longfellow's poem *Hiawatha* Baroness Emilie von Tiesenhausen-Manteuffel asked Clark to set to music some parts that she particularly admired. This musical painting of select scenes from Longfellow's epic appeared nine years before Dvořák's ninth symphony, "From the New World", and it is probably the first musical illustration of "Hiawatha." The three pieces were also intended as studies for the Clark-Steiniger pianoforte school. After fifteen years of use in teaching, they were finally published in 1900.

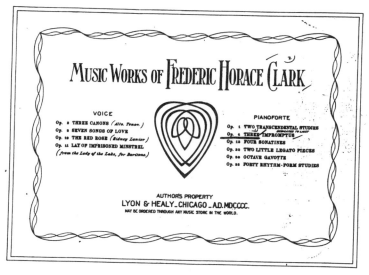

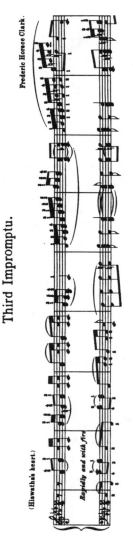
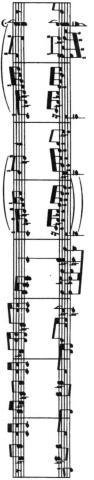
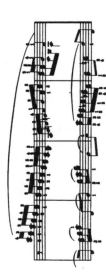

Third Impromptu.

To Miss Charlotte Sieloff, Bellevue, Idaho.

Frederic Horace Clark.

(Hiawatha's heart.)

Rapidly and with fire

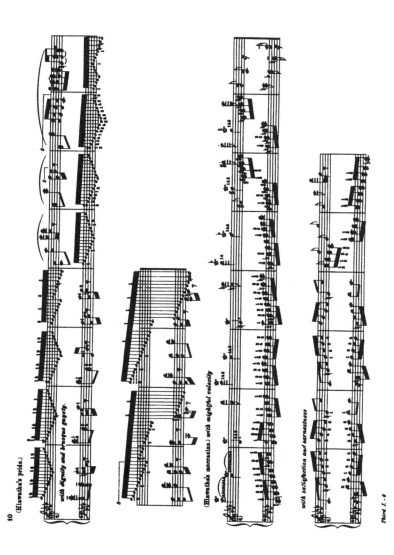

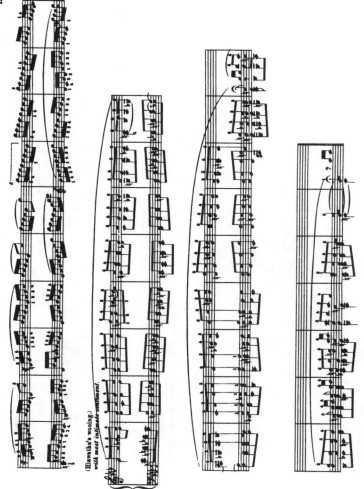

(Hiawatha's wooing.)
with most intimate sentiment.

Plate I. - 8

Appendix C

F. H. Clark's Edition of Six Etudes by Cramer

This is the only so far recovered part of the series *The Artists Unified*, with the full title: *A Poetic Edition of Six Cramer Etudes; A Series of Musical Form Etchings, Being Studies (First Group of Second Grade) in the Clark-Steiniger Pianoforte School*. Chicago: published for the Pure Music Society, copyright 1895.

The Artists Unified or Poetic Edition
OF
Classical works of Modern Instrumental Music.
BY FREDERIC HORACE CLARK.
BEING A SYMBOLIZATION OF THE SMALL AND LARGE RHYTHMS OR PARTS OF THE MUSIC
AND THEIR ENVELOPMENT IN VERSES STANZAS AND GROUPS OF STANZAS.

The Symphonies and Sonatas of MOZART, SCHUBERT and BEETHOVEN.
· THE PRELUDES AND FUGUES OF BACH · THE SONGS WITHOUT WORDS OF MENDELSSOHN ·
· THE ETUDES OF CHOPIN ·

SIX CRAMER ETUDES
Copyrighted 1895 by Frederic Horace Clark.

Copyright in 1891, by Frederic Horace Clark.

Published for the Pure Music Society, instituted through the tuition of Frederic Horace Clark. For sale by Pupils and Teachers of the Clark-Steiniger School, and at Lyon & Healy's Music Store in Chicago.

A POETIC EDITION

OF

SIX CRAMER ETUDES

A SERIES OF MUSICAL FORM ETCHINGS

BEING STUDIES (FIRST GROUP OF SECOND GRADE) IN THE

CLARK-STEINIGER PIANOFORTE SCHOOL

Published for the PURE MUSIC SOCIETY

Instituted through the Tuition of Frederic Horace Clark

FOR SALE BY PUPILS AND TEACHERS OF THE CLARK-STEINIGER SCHOOL AND ALSO AT

LYON & HEALY'S MUSIC STORE IN CHICAGO

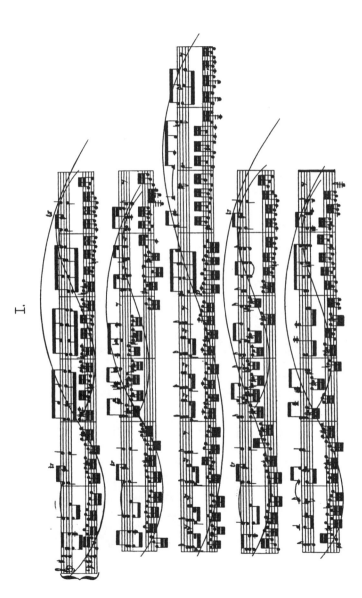

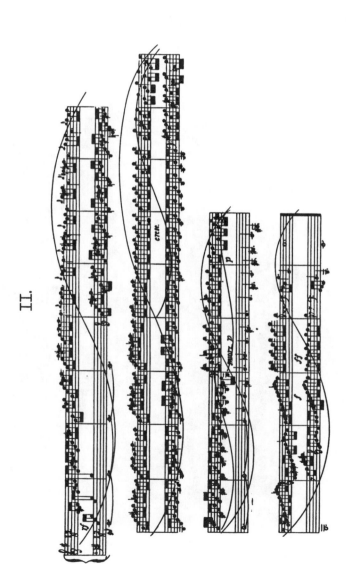

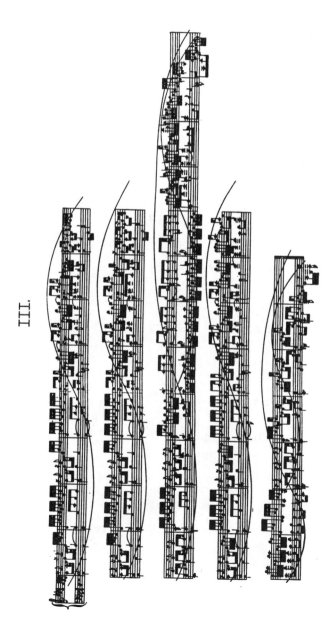

IV.

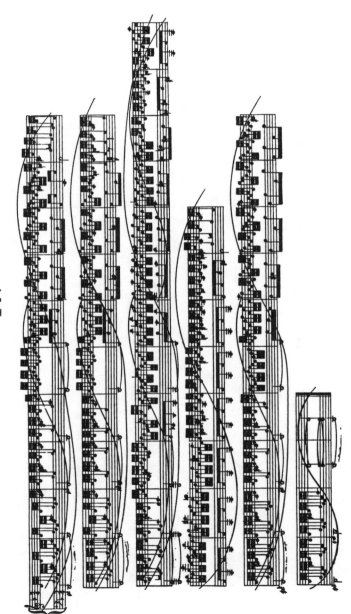

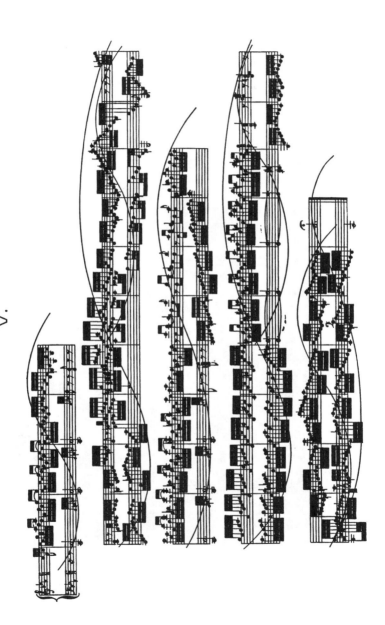

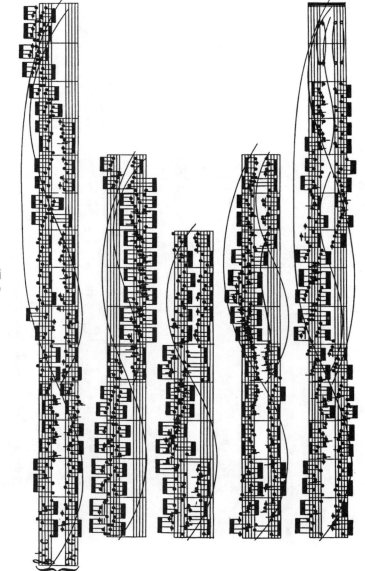

Bibliography

Works of Frederic Horace Clark

Books and Articles

The Artists Unified or Poetic Edition of Classical Works of Modern Instrumental Music, by Frederic Horace Clark; Being a Symbolization of the Small and Large Rhythms or Parts of the Music and Their Envelopment in Verses, Stanzas, and Groups of Stanzas; The Symphonies and Sonatas of Mozart, Schubert and Beethoven; the Preludes and Fugues of Bach; the Songs Without Words of Mendelssohn; the Etudes of Chopin. Another subtitle, appearing above the introductory page of the series, reads: A Harmonic Analysis of the Prime Features of the Musical Art-Organism. The only so far recovered part of the series is in the New York Public Library, and bears the title *A Poetic Edition of Six Cramer Etudes; A Series of Musical Form Etchings, Being Studies (First Group of Second Grade) in the Clark-Steiniger Pianoforte School.* Chicago: published for the Pure Music Society, copyright 1895. MGG indicates 1891 as the year, which is true if it pertains to the beginning of the series, but Clayton F. Summy as the publisher.

The following four works pertaining to this series are quoted at the end of the *Music of the Future and of the Present* Vol. 1 No. 3 (December 1901), following the advertisment for Clark's "Eight Grand Concerts of Pianoforte Music" (see Appendix A), after page 228, under the title *Musical Works and Books on Musical Art by Frederic Horace Clark for sale by the author, 1004 Steinway Hall, Chicago, U. S. A.* (quoted as in the original):

Artists' Unified Editions in Form of Etchings

Beethoven's Tenth Sonata—eight etchings
Beethoven's Moonlight Sonata—seven etchings
Cramer—Six Etudes—six etchings
Bach—Two Inventions—six etchings

"Beethoven Sonata Pastorale (op. 28)." *Music* 15 (January 1899): 304-11.

Brahms' Noblesse. Zürich: Pianistenharmoniepresse, 1914.

Ein alter Brief an Liszt (Über das wahre Legatospiel). Reprint by C. G. Röder, Leipzig, from *Musikalisches Wochenblatt* (Leipzig, 30. August 1906). The letter itself is dated "Berlin-London, February 1883."

Heaven or America: The Pope and Christ. N.p.: Society of the Sacred Heart, 1898.

"Impressions of Beethoven's Sonatas: The Two Sonatas, op. 27, nos. 1 and 2; 'Fantasie' Sonata and 'Moonlight' Sonata." *Music* 1 (January 1892): 243-63.

"Impressions of Beethoven's Sonatas: Sonata in D minor, op. 31; Sonata in F major, op. 54." *Music* 1 (February 1892): 368-93.

Iphigenia, Baroness of Styne. London: Pure Music Society, priv. ed., 1896. (Published under the name Frederic Clark-Steiniger)

Die Klasizität des Musizierens: 3 Schönheits-Idyllen von St.Damian. Berlin: Schnürpel, 1907. (self-published) As found in MGG, s.v. "Clark, Frederic Horace."

Die Lehre des einheitlichen Kunstmittels beim Klavierspiel. Berlin: Raabe & Plotow, 1885. (Published as Frederic Clark-Steiniger)

Liszts Offenbarung: Schlüssel zur Freiheit des Individuums. Berlin: C. F. Vieweg, 1907.

Music of the future and of the Present, Chicago 1901ff; continued as *Das Musizieren der Zukunft* (vols. 21-28). Pianistenharmonie-presse.

On "Religious Education in Our Schools," and the Christian Teaching of Music, Particularly Pianoforte Music: A Plea to Leo XIII. Chicago and Valparaiso, Ind.: n.p., 1897.

"The Philosophy of Pianoforte Music." Chapters 1-3 in *Music* 1 (April 1892): 613-20; chapters 4-5 in *Music* 2 (May 1892): 98-104.

"A Poetic Edition of Beethoven's 'Moonlight' Sonata: A Series of Etchings by Frederic Horace Clark." Chicago: Clayton F. Summy, 1892 (?). Discussed in a review in *Music* 1 (April 1892): 621-2. One page, probably from this edition, is reproduced in *Iphigenia,* and so far is the only one recovered.

"Sonata Characteris[ti]que (op. 81[a])." *Music* 15 (February 1899): 431-37.

Compositions

All of these compositions are listed as shown on the title page of *The Red Rose,* published by Clayton F. Summy. The company, now Summy-Birchard, and a subsidiary of Warner Publishing Company, has no record of Clark or his works.

Op. 1   Two Transcendental Studies for piano (dedicated to Liszt).
Op. 3   Three Canons (Alto, Tenor).
Op. 4   Three Impromptus for piano. Chicago: Lyon and Healy, 1900.
Op. 8   "Seven Songs of Love."
Op. 10   "The Red Rose" for voice. Chicago: Clayton F. Summy "for the author" (self-published?), Chicago, 1900.

Op. 11   "Lay of Imprisoned Minstrel" for baritone.
Op. 13   Four Sonatines [*sic*] for piano.
Op. 20   "Octavo gavotte" for piano.
Op. 22   Two Little Legato Pieces for piano.
Op. 25   Forty Rhythm-form Studies for piano.

The following original works by Clark pertaining to the above-mentioned *Artists' Unified Editions in Form of Etchings* series appear at the end of the *Music of the Future and of the Present* Vol. 1 No. 3 (December 1901), following the advertisment for Clark's "Eight Grand Concerts of Pianoforte Music" (quoted as in the original):

First Sonata Scherzo—four etchings
Minstrels' Lay—six etchings [see Clark's Op. 11 above]

The following original works by Clark appear in the above-mentioned list under the title *Original Compositions Engraved*:

Three Impromptus for pianoforte [see Op. 4 above]
Octave Gavotte for pianoforte [see Op. 20 above]
Two Legato Pieces for pianoforte [see Op. 22 above]
Forty Rhythm-Form Studies for pianoforte [see Op. 25 above]
The Red Rose for voice and piano [see Op. 10 above]
Love's Eyes for voice and piano
Not Yet for voice and piano
The Eyes of My Love for voice and piano

General Bibliography

Andres, Robert. "Frederic Horace Clark: A Forgotten Innovator." *Journal of the American Liszt Society* 27 (January-June 1990): 3-16.

_____. "Frederic Horace Clark: A Forgotten Innovator." M.M. thesis in musicology, University of Kansas, 1992.

_____. "Cherubim-doctrine," *Harmonie-piano*, and Other Innovations of Frederic Horace Clark." D.M.A. document, University of Kansas, 1993.

Breithaupt, Rudolf M. *Die natürliche Klaviertechnik*. 3rd ed. Leipzig: C. F. Kahnt Nachfolger, 1912. 1st ed., 1905.

Cobb, John Storer. *Anna Steiniger, a Biographical Sketch: In Which Is Contained a Suggestion of the Clark-Steiniger System of Pianoforte Playing*. Boston: Schirmer, 1886.

Engel, Karl Wilhelm. "*Liszts Offenbarung* als Wegweiser zu einer naturgemäßen Körpermechanik des Klavierspieles." Reproduced as manuscript, preface signed Vienna, July 1972. Universitäts-bibliothek, Vienna.

Fay, Amy. *Music Study in Germany*. Chicago: Jansen, McClurg, 1880.

Hamburger, Klára. *Liszt*. Budapest: Corvina, 1987.

A Handbook of American Music and Musicians, 1886 ed. Reprint, New York: Da Capo Press, 1971. S.v. "Steiniger-Clark, Anna."

Leibnitz, Gottfried Wilhelm von. *Monadology*. Trans. George Martin Duncan. New Haven: Tuttle, Morehouse & Taylor, 1890.

Mathews, W. S. B., ed. "Editorial Bric-a-brac" *Music* 1 (January 1892), 5 (October 1900).

Die Musik in Geschichte und Gegenwart. S.v. "Clark, Frederic Horace," by Kurt Johnen.

Muzička enciklopedija. Zagreb: JLZ, 1971-77. S.v. "Clark, Frederic Horace."

The New Encyclopedia of Music and Musicians. New York: Macmillan, 1939. S.v. "Clark, Frederic Horace."

The New Grove Dictionary of Music and Musicians (1980). S.v. "Keyboard," by Nicolas Meeus.

Ortmann, Otto. *The Physiological Mechanics of Piano Technique*. New York: Dutton, 1929. Reprint, 1962.

Ott, Bertrand. *Liszt et la pedagogie du piano*. Issy-les-Moulineaux: Editions scientifiques et psychologiques, 1978. English language version, adapted, *Lisztian Keyboard Energy* (Lewiston, N.Y.: Edwin Mellen, 1992).

Steinhausen, Friedrich Adolf. *Über die physiologischen Fehler und die Umgestaltung der Klavier-Technik*. Leipzig: Breitkopf und Härtel, 1905.

_____. *Die Physiologie der Bogenführung*. Leipzig: Breitkopf und Härtel, 1903.

The 20th Century Biographical Dictionary of Notable Americans. Boston: Biographical Society, 1904. S.v. "Clark, Horace Francis."

Walker, Bettina. *My Musical Experiences*. London: Bentley, 1890. 2nd ed., 1892.

Index

Bold entries contain the most relevant information on a particular topic.

Agthe, Albrecht Wilhelm Johann, 29
Albert, Eugène d', 116, 124
Alcott, Amos Bronson, 10
Allgemeine Musikzeitung, 9
Alps, the, 3
America (United States), 4, 5, 6, 9, 11, 12, 13, 27, 30, 37, 49, 86, 125, 127
American Protective Association, 43
Anna Steiniger, a Biographical Sketch, 27
Aristotle, 58
    entelechy, 48
    "harmony-problem no. 38," 58
Arnim, Bettina von, 8

Bach, J. S., 1, 49, 89, 91, 113
Balakirev, Miliy, 98
Bandmann, Antonia, 8, 11, 12, 106, 107, 108, 114
    Weight Technique, 108
Barth, Max, 13, 104
Bayreuth, 7
Beethoven, L. van, 1, 7, 8, 87, 89, 110, 112, 114, 120
    Concerto no. 4, 30
    Concerto no. 5, 29
    Eroica variations, 30
    "Moonlight Sonata," 2
    Piano Sonatas Op. 27, Op. 28, Op. 31 no. 2, Op. 54, Op. 81a, 86-89
Berlin, 7, 12, 13, 30, 44, 45, 77, 122
    Bechstein Hall, 12
    Beethoven Hall, 105
    Hochschule für Musik, 13
    Royal Academy, 13
    Singakademie, 12, 66, 114
    University, 8, 13, 115
Bismarck, Otto von, 60
Boissier, Auguste, 121

Bomberger, E. Douglas, 120
Bormio (Bad), 3
Boston, 9, 10, 107
    Chickering Hall, 31
    Evening Traveler, 112
    Music Hall, 30
    New England
    Conservatory,
    89
    Symphony Orchestra, 30,
    31
Brahms, Johannes, 48, 49, 50,
    75, 76, 100, 127
Brandt, John L., 43
Breithaupt, Rudolf Maria, 12,
    69, 70, 71, 106, 107, 108,
    109, 114
    *Die natürliche
    Klaviertechnik*, 69, 70
Brenner Pass, 3
Bulow, Hans von, 104
Bull, Ole, 112
Busoni, Feruccio, 105, 120

Cady, Calvin B., 89
Caland, Elisabeth, 37, 70, 108,
    109, 114, 121, 125
    *Ausnutzung der
    Kraftquellen beim
    Klavierspiel, Die*, 108
Carreño, Teresa, 105
*Charlottenburg
Intelligenz-Blat*, 8
cherubim, 55, 56, 57
"Cherubim-doctrine," 12, 56,
    78
Chicago, 1, 2, 4, 6, 9, 11, 14,
    30
    Newberry Library, 95
    Stevan School, 88
Chopin, Fryderyk, 29, 65, 105,

110, 112, 120
Christian Science, 31
Clark, Frederic Horace
    Artists Unified, The, 93
    Brahms' Noblesse, 7, 11,
    12, 14, **48-50**, 65, 75, 76,
    78, 89, 90
    *Des Christen
    Pianistenharmonie*, 14
    Ein alter Brief an Liszt, 44
    VI *Eudämonie Legende*, 14
    *Heaven or America: The
    Pope and Christ*, 43
    Iphigenia, 6, 9, 27, 28, 30,
    31, **40-42**, 57, 83
    *Lehre des einheitlichen
    Kunstmittels beim
    Klavierspiel, Die*, 9, **37-
    40**, 57, 61, 65, 66, 70,
    75, 79, 81
    Liszts Offenbarung, 2, 4, 5,
    45-47, 48, 60, 68, 75, 89,
    92, 106, 114, 119, 120,
    121, 122
    *Music of the Future and of
    the Present*, 14, 103, 104
    Das Musizieren derZukunft,
    14, 103
    *On Religious Education in
    Our Schools*, 43
    *Philosophy of Pianoforte
    Music, The*, 61, **83-89**, 94
    Pianistenharmonie, **47-48**,
    65, 76, 83
    Pianistenharmonie II, 14
    Pianistenharmoniepresse,
    14, 50
    Three Impromptus Op. 4,
    95-101
Cobb, John Storer, 7, 27, 28,
    30, 31
Cramer, Johann Baptist, 89,

90, 92

Crysdale, Mr., 31

Czerny, Karl, 29, 89

Dalcroze, Emile Jacques, 92

Darwin, Charles, 61

David, 50

Deppe, Ludwig, 4, 5, 6, 7, 8,
29, 30, 46, 47, 49, 97, 106,
107, 108, 109, 122, 127
*Armleiden des
Klavierspielers*, 8

Detroit Conservatory of Music,
66, 104, 107

Dryden, John
"A Song for St. Cecilia's
Day, 1687", 59

Dubuque, Iowa
Santa Clara's Academy,
88, 111

Düsseldorf, 30

Dvořák, Antonin, 97

Dwight, John Sullivan, 10

Dwight's Journal of Music, 10

Ehrlich, Heinrich, 5, 6, 107
Wie übt man am Klavier,
37

Engel, Karl Wilhelm, 108
*"Liszts Offenbarung" als
Wegweiser zu einer
naturgemäßen
Körpermechanik des
Klavierspieles*, 122

"envelopment," 84

Eucken, Rudolf, 9

Eutonie, 8, 106

Faelten, Carl, 89

Fay, Amy, 6, 104, 106, 107,
120, 121
Music Study in Germany, 6,
106

Fincke, Max, 115

Foster, Stephen, 98

Frederic the Great, 28

Geißler, Friedrich Jacob Kurt,
*Philosophie des
Unendlichen*, 59

Gericke (Gayritey), Wilhelm,
30

Germany, 2, 4, 5, 10, 11, 27,
30, 125, 127

Gerster, Etelka, 30

Globe Quarterly Review, 112

God, 55, 56, 59

Godowsky, Leopold, 111, 120

Goethe, Johann Wolfgang von,
8, 59, 113

Grell, Edward, 29

Grimm, Gisela, 8

Grimm, Hermann, 8

Gross, Prof., 29

Hahn, Jakob, 66, 104

Hamburg, 6, 49

Harmonie, 12, 13, 45, 48, 57,
58, 59, 60, 61, 71, 75, 77, 115

Harmonie-method, 48

Harmonie-piano, 12, 48, **75-81**

Heinrich, Anthony Philip
*Dawning of Music in
Kentucky, The*, 97

Helmholtz, Hermann, 8, 37,
65, 69
Wirbeltheorie, 59

Hesse, Elsa, 122

Heuss, Dr., 113

Hezekial, 57
Hönng, 13
Howe, Mark Anthony De
  Wolfe, 119
*Hundred Years of Music in
  America, A*, 27

*Internationale
  Musikgeschichtliche Zeitung*,
  105
Isidor of Seville, 59
Italy, 3, 6

Jaël-Trautmann, Marie, 121
Jena, 9, 79, 115
  Gesangverein, 12
Jesus, 56
Joachim, Joseph, 13
Johnen, Kurt, 70, 119
Jones, F. P., 119

Kaemper Gerd,
  Techniques Pianistiques,
  120
Kahnt, Christian Friedrich, 3
Kassel
  Fridericianum, 12
Kaweah Colony, 31
Kempff, Wilhelm, 13
Klein, A. C., 111
Krause, Walter, 122
Kretzschmar, August
Ferdinand
  Hermann, 13
Kullak, Theodore, 29, 106, 115
Kuypers, Aafke, 30

Lachmund Carl, 119, 124

Leibniz, Gottfried Wilhelm, 47
Leipzig, 2, 4, 12
  Conservatory, 5, 66
  Gewandhaus, 30, 105
Leipziger neueste Nachrichten,
  113
Leipziger Volkszeitung, 113
Lessmans Zeitung, 8
Liebeshain, 1, 2
Liszt, Franz, 3, 4, 6, 7, 8, 12,
  38, 44, 45, 46, 47, 60, 61, 68,
  69, 71, 75, 92, 97, 99, 100,
  106, 110, 113, 115, 119, 120,
  121, 122, 123, 126, 127
    *Grande Galop
    chromatique*, 2
Livonia, 8
London, 7, 44
Longfellow, Henry Wadsworth
  Hiawatha, 95

Maas, Louis, 2
Magdeburg, 28
Mason, William, 106, 121
Mathews, W. S. B., 6, 9, 10,
  11, 76, 88, 95, 103, 107, 109,
  111, 119
Matthay, Tobias, 122
Mendelssohn, Felix, 1
Merkel, Paul, 113
Milan, 3
Monte Stelvio, 3
Moses, 56
Moszkowski, Moritz, 6
Mozart, W. A., 1, 2, 29
Munich, 3
Münsterberg, Hugo, 13
Music, 10, 27
Musikalisches Wochenblatt,
  112
Musik in der Geschichte und

Gegenwart, Die, 70, 119

Naples, 4, 7
Neue Zeitschrift für Musik,
  108, 112
New England Women's Club,
  10
Newhall, Emily, E. J. F., 10
New York, 9, 106
Niemann, Walter, 108
  Klavierlexikon, 119, 122
Noble, Sarah E., 89
Northern Indiana Normal
  School, 11

Ortmann, Otto, 80, 81, 100
  *Physiological Mechanics of
  Piano Technique*, 71, 80
Ostborne-Paulin, Waltraut, 122
Ott, Bertrand, 120, 127
  Lisztian Keyboard Energy,
  108, 121

Paderewski, Ignaz, 106
Paine, John Knowles, 98
Passo di Stelvio, 3
Paul, Oscar, 2, 4, 5, 6, 7, 66
Pembauer, Prof., 105
phorolyse, 38, 67
Pianistenharmonie, 12, 50
*Pianistische Anschlag,
  Methode und Theorie des
  Prof. Paul Pichier, Der*, 122
Pichier, Paul, 122
Pittsburgh, Pa., 1, 2, 6
Plaidy, Louis, 66
Plato, 47, 48, 58
Plotinus, 58
Potsdam, 29

Pratt, Waldo Selden, 119

Raff, Joachim
  Tageszeiten, 30
Raif, Oscar, 6
Reinecke, Carl, 30
Reuleaux, Franz, 8
  Kynematics, 8
Reuss, Prince of, 30
Revista Musical Italiana, 28
Riga, 8, 30, 95
Roës, Paul, 121
  *Music, the Mystery and the
  Reality*, 120
Rollbewegung, 72
Rollung, 69
Rome, 3, 4
Rubinstein, Anton, 38, 49, 69
Ruskin, John, 3
Russia, 27, 95

Schimon-Regan, Anna, 30
Schleinitz, Prof., 2
Schnabel, Artur, 91
Schumann, Clara, 66
Shumway, Stanley, 91
Sloane, Prof., 13
Smolian, Arthur, 113
Socrates, 55
Sorrento, 4
Spohr, Ludwig, 46
Stein (Styne) Fritz, 28, 29
Stein (Styne) Julia, 28
Stein (Styne) Maximilian, 28
Steinhausen, Friedrich Adolf,
  11, 12, 70, 107, 108, 114,
  122, 125
Steiniger, Anna, 5, 6, 7, 8, 9,
  10, 11, **27-31**, 106, 108
Stettin, 28

Steuer, Wilhelm, 76
Stoddard, Charles Warren, 27
Stradal, August, 121
Stumpf, Carl, 114
Switzerland, 13, 66, 77

Tartu, 6
Teichmüller, Gustav, 6
  Neue Psychologie, 6
  Philosophie der Liebe, 6
  *Philosophie der
    Unsterblichkeit*, 6
Thorne, W. H., 112
Tiesenhauser-Manteuffel,
  Emilie von (Countess de
  Matuschka), 8, 30, 95
Trafoi, 3

Ulrich of Strassburg, 59
Uxbridge, 9

Valparaiso, Indiana, 11
  Northern Indiana Normal
  School, 88

Vienna, 28, 30
  University, 122

Wagner, Richard, 7
Walker, Alan, 119
Walker, Bettina, 1, 5, 6, 27
  My Musical Experiences, 4,
    5, 27, 119
Weimar, 4, 7, 8
Westphal, Rudolf Georg
  Hermann, 9
Wilhelm II, Emperor (Kaiser),
  12, 50, 76
Wilson, George H., 112

Yugoslav Music Encyclopedia,
  121

Zeisler, Fanny Bloomfeld, 108
*Zeitschrift der internationalen
  Musikgesellschaft*, 115
Zurich, 7, 12, 13, 14, 77
  Sihlfeld, 14

About the Author

Robert Andres was born in Varaždin, Croatia, in 1959. He began his piano lessons at an early age in Zagreb, continuing his studies at the Zagreb Music Academy, St. Petersburg State Conservatory, Vienna, and the United States. There he studied as a Fulbright scholarship recipient at the University of Kansas with the renowned Portuguese/American pianist Sequeira Costa, earning a doctor of musical arts degree in piano and a master's degree in musicology. He has also worked with distinguished teachers such as Rudolf Kehrer, Claude Frank, Peter Katin, and Pierre Sancan, and has received valuable advice from Martino Tirimo.

After teaching at the Kalamazoo College in Michigan, United States, he moved to Madeira, Portugal, where he is actively involved in a wide range of musical activities, such as teaching, concert organizing, and critical writing. Andres also maintains a busy performing career in Europe and the United States, with recent appearances in Macao and Venezuela. He has also formed a highly successful piano duo with his wife, Irish pianist Honor O'Hea, and has collaborated for the past fifteen years with the Wiener Sängerrunde choir from Vienna, Austria.

Andres's writings extend from regular contributions to the *Classical Ireland* magazine (now ceased) to musical criticisms for Madeiran newspapers and articles for various major scholarly journals and encyclopedias. During and after Croatia's war for independence, he organized several concerts in the United States benefiting war-damaged musical institutions in Croatia. His lecture-recitals include one on Portuguese romantic piano music for the 1997 EPTA

(European Piano Teachers' Association) conference in Dubrovnik, Croatia, and in 1998 he was the principal guest artist of the *Amadeus Piano Festival* in Tulsa, Oklahoma, where he presented recitals, master classes, and conferences.

Andres has been honored with many Croatian and international prizes and distinctions. Several composers, such as Ivana Lang (Croatia), Lawrence Rackley (United States), Emmanuel Dubois (United States), and Victor Costa (Portugal), have dedicated works to him. When not busy performing, writing, or traveling, Robert Andres enjoys pursuing his hobbies, which include photography, science fiction, and golf.